MISCELLANEOUS ROAD CASES

LOUDOUN COUNTY VIRGINIA 1758-1782

Loudoun County Circuit Court
Clerk of Circuit Court
Archives

Miscellaneous Road Cases
Files No. 38 to 48
Leesburg, Virginia

Roberto Costantino

HERITAGE BOOKS
2006

HERITAGE BOOKS
AN IMPRINT OF HERITAGE BOOKS, INC.

Books, CDs, and more—Worldwide

For our listing of thousands of titles see our website
at
www.HeritageBooks.com

Published 2006 by
HERITAGE BOOKS, INC.
Publishing Division
65 East Main Street
Westminster, Maryland 21157-5026

Copyright © 2003 Roberto Costantino

Other books by the author:

*Colonial Catoctin: The Fairfax Family and the Freeholders of
Piedmont Manor and Shannondale Manor, Loudoun County, Virginia
Land Book, 1743-1820, Volume One*

*The Quaker of Olden Time: The Life and Times of Israel Thompson (d. 1795)
His Land, Plantation, Mills, Tanyard & Mansion House, and the
Rise of Wheatland, Loudoun County, Virginia*

All rights reserved. No part of this book may be reproduced or transmitted in any form or by any means, electronic or mechanical, including photocopying, recording or by any information storage and retrieval system without written permission from the author, except for the inclusion of brief quotations in a review.

International Standard Book Number: 978-1-58549-854-8

OLD LOUDOUN COUNTY
COLONY OF VIRGINIA

Harper's Ferry
Payne's Ferry
Quarter Branch
Catoctin Creek
Awbrey's Ferry
Noland's Ferry
Clapham's Ferry

Frederick County
Maryland

Goose Creek
Broad Run
Sugarland Run
Great Falls
Potomac River

to Alexandria or Belle Haven

1798 Line

Difficult Run

Fairfax County

(See * West's Ordinary)

Costantino 2003

Vestal's Gap or Key's Gap
German Settlement
Catoctin Mountain
Vestal's Gap Road
Leesburg
Carolina Road
Short Hill
Hogback Mountain
Gap Spring
to Colchester
Bull Run Mountain
Bull Run

Gregory's Gap
Colchester Road
Prince William County

Williams's Gap or Snickers's Gap
Ashby's Gap
Blue Ridge

Fauquier County

N

Table of Contents

Introduction, p. VII

Miscellaneous Road Cases File No. 38, 1758-1763

1. Sorrell and others ordered to run Road, p. 1
2. Ordered Thomas Clews and others to view Road, p. 3
3. Report of the Road from Williams's Gap to Leesburg, p. 5
4. Richard Roach's Petition for a Road, p. 7
5. Report of the Road from Kirk's Mill to Leesburg, p. 9
6. Report of Road from the Potomac River to the Mountain Road, p. 11
7. Order for Mr. Fauntleroy et al to view Road, p. 13

Miscellaneous Road Cases File No. 39, 1764-1767

8. Craven Peyton's Petition for a Road, p. 15
9. Viewers' report of new Road from Broad Run to Hough's Mill, p. 17
10. Hough's relinquishment of the repair of Broad Run Bridge, p. 19
11. Report of the Road from Abel Janney's to Mahlon Janney's Mill, p. 21
12. Order for John Champ et al to view Road, p. 23
13. Viewers' Report of the bridge over Broad Run, p. 25
14. Report of Road from Trammell's Mill to Mr. Massey's; to David Smith's, p. 27
15. Report of Road from Leesburg to Lasswell's Ford, p. 29
16. Order for Col. Minor et al to view Road, p. 31
17. Report of Road from Thomas John's to the Crossroads, p. 33
18. Petition for a Road from Joseph Thomas's to Thomas John's, p. 35
19. Report of a Road from Ox Road to Lane's Store and to Lane's Mill, p. 37
20. Report of the viewers' for a Road leading from Ashby's Gap, p. 39
21. Report of the Road from Jacob Everheart's Mill to Roach's Mill, p. 41

Miscellaneous Road Cases File No. 40, 1768

22. Copy by Chas. Binns, Clerk of Court, p. 43
23. Edward Wyatt's Petition, p. 45
24. Road to be viewed from Trenary's Run to Mead's, p. 47
25. Road from Payne's Ferry, p. 49
26. Report of Road from Nich. Minor, Gent., p. 51
27. Report of Road for Mr. Thos. Chinn, p. 53
28. Report of a Road from Trenary's Run to Wm. Mead's, p. 55
29. John Lewis's Petition for a Road, p. 57
30. Gore & Ferguson's report of a Road, p. 59

Miscellaneous Road Cases File No. 41, 1769

    31. Peyton and others to view a Road, p. 61
    32. Viewers' report of Road from Leesburg & Winchester Road to Bull Run, p. 63
    33. Isaac Nichols and Gore to view a Road, p. 65
    34. Road laid out and cleared by Samuel Smith, p. 67
    35. Powell and Chinn's report of Jas. Leith's Road, p. 69
    36. Craven and others report of a Road, p. 71
    37. Petition for a Road to Israel Thompson's Mill & Co., p. 73
    38. Janney, Williams and others to view a Road, p. 76

Miscellaneous Road Cases File No. 42, 1770

    39. Order for a Road from the Loudoun Line to the Great Mountain Road, p. 78
    40. Petition for a Road to the mouth of Catoctin Creek, p. 80
    41. Petition for a Road from Kirk's Mill to be reviewed, p. 83

Miscellaneous Road Cases File No. 43, 1771

    42. Report of Road from West's Ordinary to Snickers's Gap, p. 85
    43. Brown's Petition for a Road, p. 87
    44. Hough & Co. for a Road, p. 89
    45. View Road for William Brown & Co., p. 91
    46. Samuel Love for a Road, p. 93
    47. Petition for a Road from Piney Branch to Little River, p. 95
    48. Hands to be allotted, p. 97
    49. View Road for Thomas Pursley & Co., p. 99
    50. Samuel Potts's Road to be viewed, p. 101
    51. Return for a Road from and to Potts's Mill, p. 103
    52. Return for a Road from and to Shepard's Mill, p. 105
    53. Mercer's Petition, p. 107

Miscellaneous Road Cases File No. 44, 1772

    54. Petition for a Road from Vestal and others, p. 109
    55. Road to be viewed from Thompson's Mill & Co., p. 112
    56. Road to be viewed for Thomas West, p. 114
    57. West's Road Report, p. 116
    58. Petition for a Road to Canby's Mill, p. 118
    59. Report of Road from Payne's Road to Nixon's; Thompson's Mill, p. 120
    60. Report of a Road from Israel Thompson's Mill & Co., p. 122
    61. Petition for a Road from the Blue Ridge to Leven Powell's Mill, p. 124
    62. Horsman's Petition, p. 126
    63. Report of a Road from the Valentine Quarter & Co., p. 128

Miscellaneous Road Cases File No. 45, 1773

64. Petition for a Road by Henry Michael, p. 130
65. Brown's Petition for a Road, p. 132
66. Clapham's Report of a Road, p. 134
67. Benjamin Chandler's Petition, p. 136
68. Mercer Brown and George Taverner qualified to view a Road, p. 138
69. Road to be viewed for Wm. Horseman, p. 140
70. John Orr to open a Road, p. 142
71. Petition for a Road to Mill and Church, p. 144
72. Petition for a Road from Abel Janney's to the Quaker Meetinghouse, p. 146
73. Spencer & Co. to view a Road, p. 148
74. Petition of the Vestry of Cameron Parish, p. 150
75. John Alexander's Petition for an outlet to Geo. West's Lane, p. 152
76. Report of Road on Tuscarora Creek, p. 154
77. Road viewed from Mountain Road to Triplett's & Co., p. 156
78. Road to be viewed for Simon Triplett, Gent., p. 158
79. Road to be viewed from Dawson's to Leesburg, p. 160

Miscellaneous Road Cases File No. 46, 1774

80. Road to be viewed for Mr. Gibson, p. 162
81. Road to be viewed from Mahlon Janney's Mill to Main Road, p. 164
82. Petition for a Road from Mahlon Janney's Mill through a Settlement, p. 166
83. Report of John Gibson's Road, p. 168
84. The Petition of the subscribers, p. 170
85. The way for turning a Road, p. 172
86. Vanbuskirk and others to view Road, p. 174
87. Report of Road from Drake's meadow to Leven Powell's Mill, p. 176
88. Report of a Road up the Quarter Branch, p. 178

Miscellaneous Road Cases File No. 47, 1778

89. Report of a Road from Nixon's Mill to the Road by Hough's Mill, p. 180
90. Report of Road from George Nixon's Mill to Samuel Hough's Mill, p. 182

Miscellaneous Road Cases File No. 48, 1780-1782

91. Report of Iserman's Mill Road, p. 184
92. Order view for turning the Carolina Road, p. 186
93. Report of John Dowdall's Mill Road, p. 188
94. Report of Triplett's Mill Road, p. 190
95. Order view for turning Ox Road, p. 192
96. Report of a Road from S. Triplett's Mill, p. 194

97. Jas. Coleman, Gent. and others to view Difficult Run Bridge, p. 196
98. Order view for turning the Main Road, p. 198
99. Order to view the Mountain Road to Joseph Janney's Mill, p. 200
100. The Road from Benjamin Edwards to Leesburg, p. 202
101. Report of the Road petitioned for by Joseph Lacey, p. 204
102. Petition for the Main Road from Leesburg to Winchester, p. 206
103. Turning the Main Road leading from Leesburg to Winchester, p. 208
104. Peter Carr's Petition, p. 210

Index, p. 213

INTRODUCTION

The subject of this publication is the Miscellaneous Road Cases of Loudoun County, Virginia, from the year 1758 to 1782. Within this book are transcriptions of the existing documentation of cases once before the Loudoun Old County Court and now in the custody of the Loudoun County Circuit Court, Leesburg.

When the pioneers entered the Piedmont Region of Northern Virginia the American Indian people occupied the solid ground of the earth, and had for centuries lived in this country. Through the economy of nature they had made use of certain courses affording passage from one place to another, a path, road, or a body of water. The routes taken by the early visitors and settlers were the customary lines of travel of indigenous and sojourning Native American people.

Loudoun County was made up from a portion of the Northern Neck Proprietary being the lands belonging to Thomas, Lord Fairfax and Baron Cameron. The outline of the new County was drawn from the westernmost parts of Old Fairfax County (est. 1742) and Old Cameron Parish (est. 1748). The administrative jurisdiction of Loudoun County in the Colony of Virginia came into being as a legal governmental entity in 1757, during the French and Indian War, and was named after one John Campbell, The Right Honorable Earl of Loudoun, Captain General and Governor in Chief of his Majesty's forces in North America, and one of the sixteen Peers of Scotland.

The boundaries of Old Loudoun County stretched from the mouth of Difficult Run on the Potomac River in a southerly direction to the head of Difficult Run and then still further southward in a straight line to the mouth of Rocky Run. From that spot the boundary went in a westerly direction above Bull Run and under Goose Creek to the summit of the Blue Ridge. Then northward up the Blue Ridge to the Potomac River, again, and then down the southern shore to the beginning. The boundaries were changed in 1798 when that part of the County lying east of a line from the mouth of Sugarland Run in a straight course to Carter's Mill at the confluence of Catharpin Run and Bull Run was returned to Fairfax County.

The purpose of travel and transportation is to bring people and goods to places within a limited area where they are needed in order to optimize the variety of choices and the volume of merchandise or wares. A good system of transportation minimizes unnecessary transportation and offers a change of speed and mode to fit human needs. Mobility is an integral part of agriculture, industry, finance, government, education, and recreation. A transportation system compresses the physical geography of the earth into a society whose residents share mutual interests and participation in characteristic relationships, and a common culture.

During the 18th Century the network of transportation facilities in Loudoun County was instrumental in creating efficiency in the economy and thereby accommodating growth and change. The transportation infrastructure benefited folk by providing them with a suitable outlet for people and goods. It facilitated trade and settlement from the Tidewater Region and Pennsylvania and played an essential role in the extension of trade and settlement westward over the Blue Ridge and through the Appalachian Mountain System to the Ohio River Valley, and southward through the Piedmont Region to Carolina. And, it was indispensable to the establishment and development of the town of George Town or Leesburg located on and about the intersection of the Vestal's Gap Road and the Carolina Road.

The Miscellaneous Road Cases come from the records of the Old County Court as recorded by Charles Binns, Clerk of Court. Each one of them was written on a sheet or scrap of paper in pen and ink, usually on both sides, and signed by several different people, normally. The words of some of the cases were copied over into the Court Order Book(s). The County Court was responsible for contracting for and overseeing the development of public improvements including concerns related to circulation. They exercised legal authority over and allocated public expenditures towards travel and transportation according to the customs of the people, especially for public roadways connecting village and town, courthouse, church, bridge, ferry, gap, ford, market, and mill.

Investment into and expenses relating to transportation were a local concern. There were processes available for levying freeholders and housekeepers to raise the monies required for the job or jobs. It was not until 1786 that the State government interposed and passed an Act or Law for keeping the roads in repair from Snickers's and Vestal's Gap to Alexandria, and for erecting turnpikes thereon. They were modeled after English turnpikes and were furnished with tollgates in the form of a revolving barrier used to block a road. At the time, George Gilpin and Charles Little, Commissioners, were authorized to open the two turnpikes.

Typically, the County Justices met together to discuss and arrange what roads should be laid out and marked and which required maintenance. Also, they sought to make passable for horse and foot the various bodies of water the subject roadways crossed. In order to carry on the manual labor of clearing, making, amending and repairing of these roadways, the Court would appoint surveyors and overseers who were empowered to employ freeholders as "hands". For example, when roads were saturated and cut by wagons and carts a method of addressing the problem at hand was to put to service laborers to lay down timber poles across the road, which stuck fast in the mud and made a causeway.

Foremost in importance in Loudoun County were two places of passage that connected the Tidewater Region and port towns of Alexandria and Colchester with the Piedmont Region and the Blue Ridge. One of them known to some as the Colchester Road or Braddock Road or Mountain Road went through the Blue Ridge at Williams's Gap or Snickers's Gap in the vicinity of today's Rt. 7. The other one known as the Vestal's Gap Road or Alexandria Road or Braddock Road, again, went through the Blue Ridge at Vestal's Gap or Key's Gap about where Rt. 9 now runs. The subject roadways were delineated in a 1754 Edition of John Warner's 1737 Map of the Northern Neck. Additionally, there were other principal routes through the Blue Ridge at Ashby's Gap near present day Rt. 50 and Gregory's Gap near Rt. 641.

Some other old routes with an easterly-westerly aspect, more or less, included a road that meandered to and from Gum Spring along the eastern shore of Broad Run to the said Vestal's Gap Road or Alexandria Road that was known in the Colonial Period even as "Old" Ox Road (Rt. 606). There was also the Church Road by which way one could go back and forth from a Goose Creek mill-seat to Sugarland Run and beyond (Rt. 625).

As for some important passages with a northerly-southerly aspect, there was a main road that ran from the Potomac River up and down the eastern side of the Catoctin Mountain and Hogback Mountain to Bull Run and beyond, called the Carolina Road (Rt. 15: Rt. 621: Rt. 860). Another such route in the extreme northwest of the County under the Blue Ridge went from below Robert Harper's Ferry on the Potomac River and Between the Hills before it crossed Vestal's Gap Road and continued by extension all the way to Williams's Gap (Rt. 671: Rt. 719: Rt. 711). Likewise too there was a roadway under Short Hill that went north to south by extension from the Drains of Dutchman Creek and across the Vestal's Gap Road to a settlement around the Goose Creek Meeting (Rt. 852: Rt. 690: Rt. 611). Another one went up and down Catoctin Creek and South Fork thereof to a settlement in the vicinity of the Fairfax Meeting (Rt. 665). In the southwest of the County were a couple of roads that went from near Williams's Gap or Snickers's Gap back and forth in the direction of Ashby's Gap Road (Rt. 765 and Rt. 719).

There are at least three more old maps of Loudoun County or Virginia that serve to point out the state of the transportation infrastructure at a given time. One of them is the 1816 Map of Virginia by F. Lucas published in Baltimore. A second is the Woods/Boye Map of 1827/1859. The largest in scope is the Map of Loudoun County, Virginia, by Yardley Taylor published in Philadelphia, 1853. Many of the roads were nothing more than foot or bridle paths marked by the blazing of trees, that is, a chunk of wood and bark was cut out of a tree. There were, however, a few highways that were broader and passable by wagon and cart, or for rolling.

It was a custom of the time for travelers to cross the Potomac River by ferry and so to go from one place to another through Maryland, thereby accessing in a northerly direction, Frederick; in an easterly direction, Georgetown; in a westerly direction and again through Virginia to Mecklenburg or Shepherdstown. An early Ferry in Loudoun County was Clapham's. Apparently, the busiest ferry in the County was Noland's Ferry. Besides, there was Awbrey's Ferry under the mouth of Catoctin Creek. And, in the northwest portion of the County was Payne's Ferry. The ferries were operated by legal right as a commercial public service for transporting people, animals, goods, or the like, across a body of water.

The written words reflecting on the sessions of the Old County Court were reproduced including the odd sentence structure and the use of capitalization within sentences. Punctuation, remarkable for its absence, was copied as well except for a few commas and an occasional period. In all cases, however, proper names were spelled just as they were recorded. While spelling of such names varies widely throughout the records and even in the same document, no attempt was made to standardize it. As a result, its not always clear whether a name is being properly reproduced or, rather, the carelessness or ignorance of the scribe.

I'm thankful to Patty, Julie and Marc, friends and acquaintances. I'm particularly indebted to the Office of the Clerk of Circuit Court for their valuable assistance. I'm appreciative of benefits received from the Thomas Balch Library, Leesburg, and, specifically, from Eugene M. Scheel, for his historical maps. I hereby express my gratitude and thanks.

Roberto Costantino

Miscellaneous Road Cases File No. 38, 1758 to 1763
Clerk of Circuit Court
Archives
Leesburg, Virginia

Loudoun County   October Court 1758

    Ordered that Thomas Sorrell Benjamin Grayson G[t] and William Ross being first Sworn before a Justice of the Peace of this County do run the most convenient way for a Road leading from George Town to Vincent Lewis's Road and make report thereof to the Court.

Loudoun Sc
    The above Persons was   A Copy
    Sworn before Nich Minor   Teste
Octo[r] 24th 1758
                          Cha[s] Binns Cl Cur

(over)

        Sorrell & others Ord[r]
          to run Road

Loudoun Sc

    Pursuant to the within Order the Subscribers have viewed for y[e] within mentioned Road w[ch] we judge should be as follows viz. From George Town along the new Road to a glade between John Moss and Tho[s] Sorrell, then leaving said Road & running near in a straight line to y[e] east end of Benj[n] Shreeve's Plantation, thence to ye same end of W[m] Shreeve's Plantation thence to y[e] west end of J[no] Dawson's Plantation, to Dawson's Ford thence along an old Road by M[r] Elzey's Plantation & so by Vincent Lewis. Given under our hands this 14 of Nov[r] 1758.

                Benj. Grayson   Tho[s] Sorrell
                                       W[m] Ross

Road Case File # 38   1758-1763
Loudoun County Circuit Court

Loudoun County   October Court 1758

Ordered that Thomas Sewell Benjamin Grayson & Mr William Ross
being first sworn before a Justice of the Peace do view the nearest & most
convenient way for a Road leading from George Town down Sorrels Road
and make Report thereof to the Court

Loudoun ss
                                                         Teste
The above Persons were   Cha[s] Binns Cl[k]
                    Sworn before Rich[d] Brown
Octo[r] 24th 1758

                        1758
                Sorrells & others ord[r]
                    Sorrell Road

Loudoun ss
            Pursuant to the within order the Subscribers
have viewed the within mentioned Road w[hich] we Judge should
be as follows viz: from George Town along the new road to
a Glade between John Moss and Tho[s] Sorrells, Then leaving said
road & running Near in a Strait line to y[e] East end of Benj[a]
Sheeves Plantation, thence to y[e] same End of W[m] Sheeves Plantation
thence to y[e] West End of the Lawsons plantation, to Lawsons ford &
thence along an old Road by ind[?] Elzey's plantation &c so by Vincent Lewis's
Given under our hands this [th] of [Oct] 1758 Benj[a] Grayson Tho[s] Sorrell
                                                                W[m] Ross

Loudoun County	June Court 1759

Ordered that Thomas Clews Francis Wilks Jeremiah Fairhurst and William Janney or any three thereof being first sworn before a Justice for this County view the most convenient way for a Road from Williams's Gap to Leesburgh and mark the same and make Report thereof to the Court.

	A Copy
		Teste
			C Binns Cl Cur

(over)

Loudoun Sc

	This day Thomas Clews Francis Wilks & Jeremiah Fairhurst was duly qualified according to Law to View according to the within Order Certified under my hand this 31st day of July 1759

			Nich Minor

Ord^r Thom^s Clews & oth^s
to View Road

Road Case File # 38 1758-1763
Loudoun County Circuit Court
Leesburg, Virginia

Loudoun County   June Court 1759

Ordered that Thomas Glenn, Francis Wilks, Jeremiah Fairhurst and
William Janney or any three thereof being first sworn before a Justice for this
County view the most convenient way for a Road from William's Gap to
Leesburgh and mark the same and make Report thereof to the Court

                                              A Copy Teste C Binns Clerk

Loudoun So This day Thomas Glenn, Francis Wilks &
Jeremiah Fairhurst were Duly Qualified
According to Law to View According to the
Within Order Certifyed under my hand this
31st day of July 1759

Pursuant to an Order of June Court 1759
we the Subscribers have viewed and marked
the way from William's Gap to Leesburg
and are of opinion that the most suitable
way for a Road to be as followeth
To turn out of the old Road at some marked
trees at the foot of the Mountain near
Comptons Path, thence by the South end of
the Round Hill, thence a direct course
from their to Nathan Spencer's and from
their to Jacob Janney's Mill thence a direct
course into the Great Road near R. Canarys.

Promise to pay

(over)

A Report of the Road
from William's Gap
to Leesburgh.

Road Case File # 38   1758-1763
Loudoun County Circuit Court
Leesburg, Virginia

Pursuant to order of June Court
1759 we the Subscribers have viewed
and Mar[k]t
the way from Williams Gap to Leesburg
and are of Opinion that the most Suit=
=able way for a Road to be as followeth.
To turn of the old Road at Somemarks
tree at the foot of the Mountain
near Campton's path, Thence by the
South end of the Round hill, thence a Direct
Course from there to Nathan Spencers
& from there to Jacob Janny's Mill
and from thence a Direct Course
into the Great Road Near R[d]. Eneary's

To the Worshipful the Court of Loudoun County._____
The Petition of Richard Roach humbly showeth that
his Mill is now finished and in order for grinding of
grain & and has no Road opened to s^d Mill fit for
carriages._____ Your Petitioner therefore humbly
prays that he may have a Road from William Kirks
Road near Richd Roberts to s^d Mill and from thence to the
locust thicket the most convenient way and your Petiti^r
as in duty bound shall ever pray &_____

(over)

Richd Roach's Pet^o
for a Road

Road Case File # 38   1758-1763
Loudoun County Circuit Court
Leesburg, Virginia

To the Worshipfull the Court of Loudoun County

The Petition of Richard Roach Humbly Sheweth that
his Mill is now finished and in order for Grinding of
Grain & and hath no Rode opened to s.d Mill for the
Carriage ——— your Petitioner therefore Humbly
prays that he may have a Rode from William Hawkins
Rode near Rich.d Roberts to s.d mill and from thence to the
Bear thicker the most convenient way and your Petit.r
as in duty bound shall ever pray &

Whereas there was an Order issued from this Court some time ago directed to us the Subscribers requiring us to View & Report, the best way for a Road to be got from Wm Kirks Mill to this place. We being well acquainted with the situation of the lands recommend that a Road be br^t along by Ralf Braddocks thence to Richd Roberts's & thence with a straight course to a Bridge in the Main Road nigh Robt Popkins's Fence (above Popkins Plant.)

        June 9th Josias Clapham
        1761   John Trammell

(over)

Viewers Report of the
Road from Kirk's Mill
to Leesburgh
June 9, 1761
Road to be cleared

Road Case File # 38   1758-1763
Loudoun County Circuit Court
Leesburg, Virginia

Whereas there are an [illegible] from the Court sometime ago issued to us the several Regimers as to the of Report, the best way for us to do it from Wm Fees will be this know we being well acquainted with the Organization of the Lands Surveyors that a Road be laid along by Robt Bullocks Hoose to Redi Robt: I think with a straight line to adbridge in the Soams and from Boot Stephens Road (and Stephens that

Jonas Clapham
1761   John Trammell

These are to acquaint ye Honorable Gentlemenn of the Bench that we have upon Oath looked over and marked out a way for a Road leading from Potomack River to ye Mountain Road between ye Blue Ridge and Short Hill to the best of our skill and knowledge both for good ground and convenience of ye inhabiters.

August ye 8th 1761   Robert Yeldell
                            Nicholas Osborn

(over)

Rept of Road from Potomk
River to the Mountain
Road

Augt 19, 1761 Retd

Road Case File # 38 1758-1763
Loudoun County Circuit Court
Leesburg, Virginia

These are to Certify to ye Honorable Commiss[ioners?] of the Bench. that we have Surveyd (& look'd) over and open'd a way for a Road leading from Potomack River to ye Mountain (known by the name of) Blew Ridge, and from thence to the top of the said Ridge, and discovery'd a tolerable good (& sound) Conveniencey of getting into ye South Branch and August ye 8th 1763

Robert Pritchett
Nicholas Osburn

Loudoun County Sct   May Court 1763

    Ordered that Bushrod Fauntleroy Jacob Remey and Thomas Connell or any two thereof being first Sworn View the most convenient way for a Road leading from out of the Mountain Road below Mr Chas Eskridge's to Capt James Lane's Mill & from thence to the Road that leads to Prince William & make a Report of the conveniency & inconveniency that may atten the same to the Court.

                       Teste
                           Cha Binns Cl

(over)

    In obedience to t' within Order we t' Subscribers being first Sworn before James Lane one of his Majesties Justices for t' sd County have Viewed t' Roads conformable to t' within Order, & find that a Road may be Opened from t' Mountain Road to Capt Jas Lane Mill & from thence to t' Road to Prince William Court will be very convenient to t' publick & prejudice no Plantation.

                         Thos Connell
t' 8 Day Augt 1763   Jacob Ramey

Ordr per Mr Fauntleroy
& al to view Road

Road Case File # 38   1758-1763
Loudoun County Circuit Court
Leesburg, Virginia

Loudoun County Sc.   May Court 1763

Ordered that Richard Taintterey Jacob Remey and Thomas Connell or any two thereof being first sworn view the most convenient way for a Road leading from out of the Mountain Road below Michael Eldridge's to Capt. James Lane and make their Report to the Next the Head of Somon Meklam and make a Report of the Conveniency & Inconveniency that may attend the same to this Court.

                                                Test
                                                Cha: Binns C

In Obediance of within Order we Subscribers Being first sworn Before James Lane one of his Majesty's Justices for sd County have Viewed a Road Conformable to sd within Order, & Say that sd Road to ____
sd Mountain Road to Capt. Lanes ____ from ____
to sd Road to ____ will be very convenient
to ye publick & ____
sd 8 day Augt. 1763   Thos Connell
                                                Jacob Remey

14

Miscellaneous Road Cases File No. 39, 1764 to 1767
Clerk of Circuit Court
Archives
Leesburg, Virginia

To the Worshiful Court of Loudoun County
The Petition of Craven Peyton humbly prays that
the Road that leads from Lasswell's Ford to
Lee'sburg may be allowed a more convenient way
than it now is and your Petitioner shall ever
pray.

(over)

Craven Peyton's Petition for a Road

Road Case File # 39 1764-1767
Loudoun County Circuit Court
Leesburg, Virginia

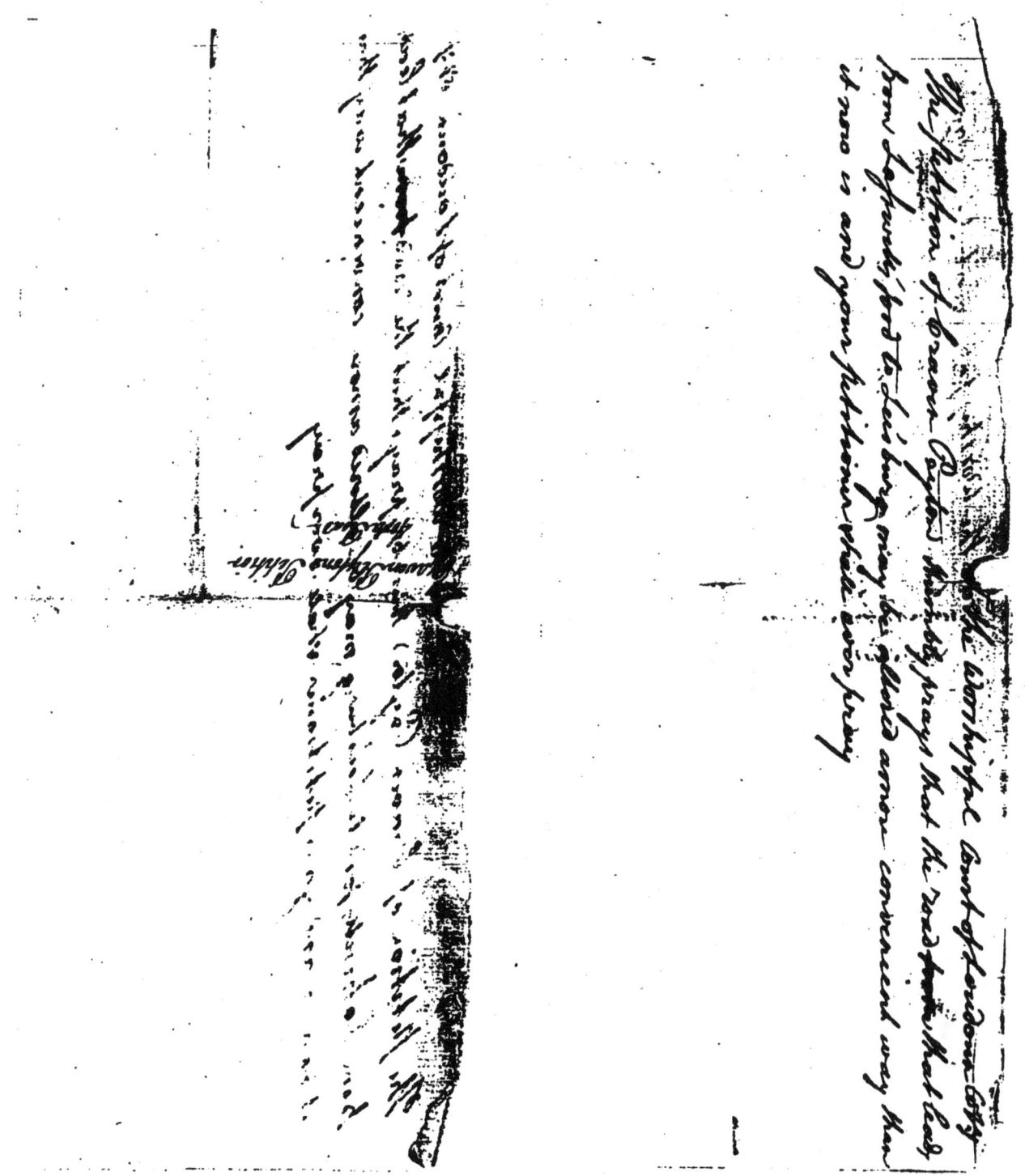

The Petition of the Inhabitants of the County of Loudoun County
Sheweth that your petitioners humbly pray that the road that leads
from Leesburg [to] Leesburg may be altered a more convenient way than
it now is and your petitioners shall ever pray

In obedience to an Order of this Court we t' Subscribers being ~~first~~ Sworn before Ja^s Lane Gen^t do find that t' one Road to be turned on a straight course from where t' s^d Road crosses Broad Run to Hough Mill will be more convenient to t' publick & will prejudice no plantation given under our hands this 10 Day of April 1764.

          James Whealey
          Richard Stephens

(over)

Viewers Report of
New Road from
Broad Run to Hough's
Mill

Road Case File # 39 1764-1767
Loudoun County Circuit Court
Leesburg, Virginia

In Obedience to an Order of this Court to us Subscribers Being directed Sworn Before Adam Smith Gent. Do hereby Report, On Oath to be Nearest and Straightest Course from where the J. Roads Cross Braddock's Road Through mill will to Morris Conner, agreeable to his Gilbert & will Go Through his plantation, Given under our hands this 10 Day of April 1764

James Wheatley
Richard Stephens

To the Worshipfull Court of Loudoun

As Maj.^r James Hamilton hath undertook the repair of
Broad Run Bridge and indemnified me from my undertak-
ing please to Levy the ninety five pounds agreed for, for
the repairing of said Bridge in said Hamilton's Name as
witness my hand and seal this ninth day of May Anno D.º 1764

           John Hough

(over)

Hough's Relinqui-
shment of the -
Repair of Bro.
Run Bridge

Road Case File # 39   1764-1767
Loudoun County Circuit Court
Leesburg, Virginia

To the Worshipfull Court of Loudoun

As Maj.r James Hamilton hath undertook the Repair of
Broad Run Bridge and demands of me Twenty Dollars
ing pursuant to Leay the Same hath Agreed for for
the Repairing said Bridge and the Same as
Witness my hand and... this Mo day of June 1764

John Hough

To the Honourable Court of Justices to be held at
Leesburgh the 12 of this instant.

    We whose Names are under written have pursuant to an Order of Court dated last April, being first legally Sworn before Squire M^{c}ilheney one of his Majesties Justices of the Peace, have viewed the Road from Abel Janney's to Mahlon Janney's Mill, and it is our judgement that the convenientist and best way is where it formerly went to Rachel Hollingsworth's then to leave the old Road and go the back side of her Plantation to the s^d Mill.

June the 8th 1764   George Norman
                                                 Jonathan Richardson
                                                 James Tobin

(over)

A Report of Road from
Abel Janney's to Mahlon
Janney's Mill

June 12, 1764   Report rec^d
& Road to be cleared & ^{c}

Road Case File # 39   1764-1767
Loudoun County Circuit Court
Leesburg, Virginia

To the honourable Court of Justices to be held at Leesburgh the 12 of this instant

We whose Names are under Written have Pursuant to an Order of Court dated last April, being first Legally Sworn before Squire McIlheney one of his Majesties Justices of the peace, have viewed the Road from Abel Janney's to Mahlon Janney's Mill, and it is our Judgment that the Convenientest and best way is where it formerly went to Rachel Hollingsworth's then to leave the old Road and go the back side of her Plantation to the sd. Mill.

June the 8th 17[illegible]

George Norman
Jonathan Richardson
James Tobin

At a Court cont^d and held for Loudoun County Oct. 10, 1764 Ordered that John Champ, William Fielder, and Jacob Reed or any two thereof being first sworn before a Justice of this County all View the most convenient way for a Road from the Road against Mr Francis Peyton's to Lasswell's Ford and make a Report of the conveniency and inconveniency that will attend the same.

      Copy Chas Binns Cl Cur

Loud^n Sc^t
  John Champ & Jacob Reed two of the above
  appointed Viewers Sworn before me this 8th
  day of Novr 1764 Francis Peyton

(over)

Order per John Champ et al
to View Road

Road Case File # 39 1764-1767
Loudoun County Circuit Court
Leesburg, Virginia

At a Court held for Loudoun County Octr 12th 1764

Ordered that John Champ, William Taylor and Jacob Reed or any two thereof being first sworn before some Justice of this County, do view the most convenient way for a Road from the Road against Mr. Francis Peyton to Leesburgh &

a guard Mr Francis Peyton to Leesburgh and make a Report to the Governour and Commissioners thereunto belonging.

Copy Cha: Binns Clk

John Champe & Jacob Reed two of the ___
___ persons Viewers Woors before me this 8th day
of Novr 1764.   Francis Peyton.

Loudoun County Sct

    Pursuant to an Order of the County of Loudoun dated the fourteenth day of this Instant We have viewed the Bridge over Broad Run undertaken by Majr James Hamilton and find the same sufficiently built and completely finished.

    Given under our hands this seventeenth day of August, 1764.

        Nich Minor
        Phil. Noland

(over)

**The Viewers
Report**

Nov. 14, 1764

**Road Case File # 39   1764-1767
Loudoun County Circuit Court
Leesburg, Virginia**

Loudoun County ss.

I Loudoun dates the foregoing agreement & an order of the Court
of Loudoun dated the foregoing agreement of this Indent. We have viewed
the Bridge over Broad Run, and conceive that the same is sufficiently
Built and completely finished agreeable to the contract

Given under our hands this
seventeenth day of August 1805.

Aaron Levere
Ohio Noland

In obedience to an Order of the Worshipful Court of Loudoun We the Subscribers have Viewed a Road from John Tramells Mill towards Mr Masseys in order to go towards Leesburgh & ___ We Report it as our opinion that a Road be opened from the said Mill nigh or with a Path already in use which goes near William Jones's from thence to a corner of Mr Lee Masseys Fence and thence with the said Path into the Road from Nolands Ferry towards Leesburgh & ___ Also in obedience to an Order of sd Court to lay off a Road from sd Mill to David Smiths We give it as our opinion that it be opened from the corner of sd Tramells Fence on the Mill up an old Path to John Listers line thence by the sd Listers line & J. Claphams line to the Ferry Road thence along the sd Road to a Path that leads to David Smiths near Wm Wollards Fence.

        Josias Clapham
        Phil Noland
        Novem. 11th 1764

(over)

A Report of Road from John Trammell's Mill towards Mr Massey and also of a Road from said Mill to David Smith ret{d}

  Nov. 14, 1764

Road Case File # 39   1764-1767
Loudoun County Circuit Court
Leesburg, Virginia

In Obedience to an Order of the Worshipfull County of Loudoun
We the Subscribers have Viewed a Road from John
Tramells Mill Towards Mr. Maseys in order to
go towards Leesburgh &c — We report it as our
opinion that a Road be opened from the said Mill
nigh or with a path already in use which
goes near William Jones's from thence to a corner
of Mr. Lee Maseys fence and thence with
the said path into the Road from Nolands Ferry
Towards Leesburgh &c ———

Also in Obedience to an Order of s'd Court to lay off
a Road from s'd Mill to David Smiths — We give
it as our opinion that it be opened from the corner of s'd
Tramells fence at the Mill up an old path to
John Lesleys line thence by the s'd Lesleys line
& J. Claphams line to the Ferry Road thence along
the s'd Road to a path that leads to David Smiths
near Wm. Wollards fence ———

Josias Clapham
Phil Noland
Novemr. 11th 1764

28

Pursuant to an Order of Court Dated the fourteenth of April 1766. We the Subscribers being first Sworn before Craven Peyton Gent have been part of two days Viewing a Road agreeable to said Order, & we find if the Road leads under the Mountain, agreeable to the intent of Mr Peytons Petition, twill be attended with the inconveniency of deal of swampy ground, that must be causeway'd, & much to the prejudice of several people, & very little if any nearer than the old Road, & upon the whole we cant find that the Road can be with any conveniency altered.

        William Cotton
        Geo. Taylor
        Thos Lewis
        William Whitely

(over)

Report of Road from
Leesburg to Lasswells
Ford

June the 9th retd & Quashed

Road Case File # 39 1764-1767
Loudoun County Circuit Court
Leesburg, Virginia

At a Court held for Loudoun County April the 14th 1766

Ordered that Nicholas Minor Gent. John Moss, William Mead and Francis Wilks or any three thereof being first sworn before a Justice of this County do View the most convenient way for a Road from Thomas Starks's to William Mead's and whether it be necessary that such a Road should be cleared and make a Report of the conveniency & inconveniency that may attend the same to the Court.

          Teste Chas. Binns Cl Cur

(over)

Loudoun Sct Pursuant to the within Order We the Subscribers have Viewed the Road mentioned & are of opinion there is not any other way showed to us that is so convenient or good as the Road now used whereof John Jones is Surveyor Given under our hands this 8th day of Sept. 1766.

         Nich Minor
         John Moss
         Wm Mead

(over)

Order per Col? Minor & all to
View Road

Sept. 1766 Rept retd.
& Ord per old Road be contd.
as it now stands

Road Case File # 39 1764-1767
Loudoun County Circuit Court
Leesburg, Virginia

At a Court held for Loudoun County April the 14, 1766

Ordered that Nicholas Minor Gent, John Moss, William Mead and Francis Milhorn or any three of them being first sworn before a Justice of this County do View the most convenient way for a Road from Thomas Starks to William Mead and whether it be necessary that such a Road should be cleared and make a Report of the Conveniency & Inconveniency that may attend the same to the Court

Teste Chas Binns Clk

Loudoun ss: Pursuant to the Within Order we the Subscribers have viewed the Road mentioned & are of Opinion there is not any other way that is so convenient or good as the Road now laid whereof John Jones Surveyor Given under our hands this 8th day of Sep 1766

John Cross
Wm Mead

In obedience to an Order of Court issued at March Court that we the Viewers of the Road from Thomas Johns to the Crossroads by Joseph Thomases have Viewed the Road there in directed which we find is to run with the Line of John Todhunter and Thomas John except about thirty poles on the Land of George Going being by a Spring in the said Line which we find is as good and nearer than the old Road which we or any of us is willing to show to them who shall be appointed to open the same. Witness our hands this 21st Day March 1767.

Jos Thomas

Loudoun St March 21 Day 1767
The above Report was Sworn to before me

Abrm Dehaven

    Phil Noland

Thos George

John Steere

(over)

A Report

Road Case File # 39   1764-1767
Loudoun County Circuit Court
Leesburg, Virginia

In obedience to an order of Court Issued at March Court
that we the viewers of the Road from Thomas Johns to the Gorge Road
by Joseph Thomases have viewed the Road there in order to which
wee (is?) to begin with the line of John Tohunken and Thomas
John Except about thirty pole on the land of George Gorge
being by a Spring in the Said line which we find to be good
any futher then the old Road which we are of us is willing
to Show to them who Shall be a pointed to open the Same
Witness our hands this 28 March 1767

                                    Jos. Tilton
                                    Elijah Stevens
                                    Thos George
                                    John Reeve

Sworn to march the 28 Day 1767
The above reporte and sworn to before
me
                William Moore

To the Worshipful Court of Loudoun Coͭy

    The Petition of John Todhunter & Thomas John humbly showeth that the Road leading from Nolands Ferry & c. towards Leesburgh goes through their Lands much to their prejudice which they apprehend might be altered to go near or on their line, and be made nearer and better Road. They therefore humbly pray your Worships would relieve them by giving them leave to alter the Road or otherways as your Worships shall think proper.

                      John Todhunter
                             his
                      Thomas X John
                            mark

(over)

Petition per a Road from
Jo͡s Thomas's to Tho͡s John's
April 12, 1767 Report ret. & Ord.
per Road to be opened.

Road Case File # 39   1764-1767
Loudoun County Circuit Court
Leesburg, Virrginia

To the Worshipfull Court of Loudoun Co^ty,

The Petition of John Todhunter & Thomas John. Humbly Sheweth. That the road leading from Nolands Ferry &c. toward Leesburg goes through their lands much to their prejudice, which they apprehend might be altered to go nearer on [Kentons?] line, and be made nearer & [shorter — they therefore humbly pray your] Worships [to] relieve them by giving them leave to alter the Road or otherways as your Worships shall think proper to do

John Todhunter

Thomas ✕ John
his mark

Loudoun County

In obedience to an Order of Court to us directed we the Subscribers being first sworn before William Carr Lane Gent^Q a Justice of the Peace of this County have Viewed & find it convenient for the said Road to be cleared from Ox Road to & by the Plantation where Jno Morriss formerly lived from thence to Lanes Store & across the Mountain Road down to said Mill, & believe the said Road will not interfere with or prejudice an(y) persons plantation Certified under our hands this 11 day of April 1767.

         Benj^a Cockerill
         Sanford Cockerill
         Amos Fox

(over)

April 15, 1767 A
Report of a Road from
the Ox Road to & by the
Plantation where Jno Morris
formerly lived from thence
to Lanes Store to cross the
Main Road down to Lane's Mill
Est^d & Ordered
per same to be cleared

Road Case File # 39   1764-1767
Loudoun County Circuit Court
Leesburg, Virginia

Loudoun County

In Obedience to an order of Court here dated we
the Subscribers being first Sworn before Thomas Lewis Gent: a Justice
of the peace of the said County & Officers concerned for the said
County, have viewed from the Road to by the Church, where Charles
morgan now lives, from thence to James Hereford the nearest
and best down to, or nill, & thence the said Road will not hurt
Fine with or Injury here any Plantation, Booly, &c when our
hands this 11th day of April 1767

Benj'a Cockerill
Sanford Cockerill
Amos Fox

In obedience to an Order of the Worshipful Court of Loudoun dated August 6th 1767 have Viewed the way for the Road therein contained and are of opinion the said Road should to be taken from the big Road leading from Ashbys Gap at the upper end of Elijah Chinns old field & to be cleared a straight course from thence to a large spanish oak standing in a Branch on the Path side that leads from the s^d Chinns to George Heales Quarter supposed to be in or near the County Line, & that it may be made a convenient way & not to the prejudice of any person Witness our hands this 12th September 1767.

        Wm Stephens
        John Burk
        Jeremiah Hampton

(over)

Report of
Viewers
for a Road

Sept 14, 1767 Reported
& Road to be cleared acc.

Road Case File # 39   1764-1767
Loudoun County Circuit Court
Leesburg, Virginia

In Obediance to an Order of the worshipfull the Court of Loudoun dated August 6th 1767 have vetwed the way for the road therein contained and are of opinion the said road should to be taken from the big road leading from Ashby Gap at the upper end of Elijah Chinns Old field & to be cleared a strait course from thence to a large Spanish Oak standing in a branch on the path side that leads from the sd Chinns to George Heales Quarter supposed to be in or near the County Line, & that it may be made a convenient way & not to the prejudice of any person Witness our hands this 14th September 1767.

Wm Hutchins

John Buck

Jeremiah Hampton

According to the Order of Court that Joseph Thomas and
William Wolard and Henry Oxley Junior or any two of them
to find a Road from Jacob Everharts Mill to Richard
Rocheas Mill and we two have found a way from said
Everharts Mill up round as the Road now goes on the
reagg(?) to a white oak tree marked and then marked
through the woods near Isaac Vanbuskirk field so then
near Samuel Smiths Plantation thence along on the back
side of Nicklis Phillips field through a piece of
cleared new land and then between Adam Vincels and Henry
Topes and so from thence along by Willm Laycocks field
from thence along between Samuel Scooleys and James
Forkeson and to cross Broad Run near the Mouth of Scooleys
Spring Drain so then along the Path that leads from
Forkesons to Rocheas Mill to a Spring Drain on the said
Path so up the Drain and round the head on cross it near
the head from thence along t' old Path to the pond found
by Rocheas Mill so over to the Mill & c. this done by us.

         William Woolard
         Henry Oxley Junior

(over)

A Report of the Road from Jacob
Everheart's Mill to Roach's Mill

Novr 11, 1767 Report returned &
Road to be cleared agreeable thereto

Road Case File # 39   1764-1767
Loudoun County Circuit Court
Leesburg, Virginia

according to the order of Cort that Joseph thomas
and William Woland and Henry Oxley Junor or
two of them to find a Road from Jacob Evenharts
mill to Richard Rocheas mill and We two have
found a Way from the said Evenharts mill
up Round as the Road Now goes on the Ridge
to a White oak tree marked and then
through the Woods Near Isaac Van boskerk field
So then Near Samuel Smiths Plantation thence
along on the Back Side of Nicklis Phillips field
through a Peas of Cleared New Land and then betwin
Adam Vinselle and Henry topes and So from thence
along by Willm Saycooks feald from there along
Between Samuel Scooleys and James Jonkeson and
to Cross Broad Run Near the mouth of Scooleys
Spring Breen So then along the Path that Leads
from Jonkesons to Rocheas mill to a Spring Breen
on the said Path So up the Breen and Round the head
on Cross it Near the head from thence along the
Path to the upon found by Rocheas mill So on to
the mill this Don By us

William Woland
Henry Oxley Junor

Miscellaneous Road Cases File No. 40, 1768
Clerk of Circuit Court
Archives
Leesburg, Virginia

Loudoun Sct   March Court 1768

    On the Motion of Nicholas Minor Gent. Ordered that William Buchannan Peter Carter William Veale & James Jennings or any three of them view the most convenient way to turn a Road that is now running through the said Nicholas Minor's Plantation and report the conveniencies to the Court.

                                Copy
                                    Cha. Binns Cl.

Road Case File # 40 1768
Loudoun County Circuit Court
Leesburg, Virginia

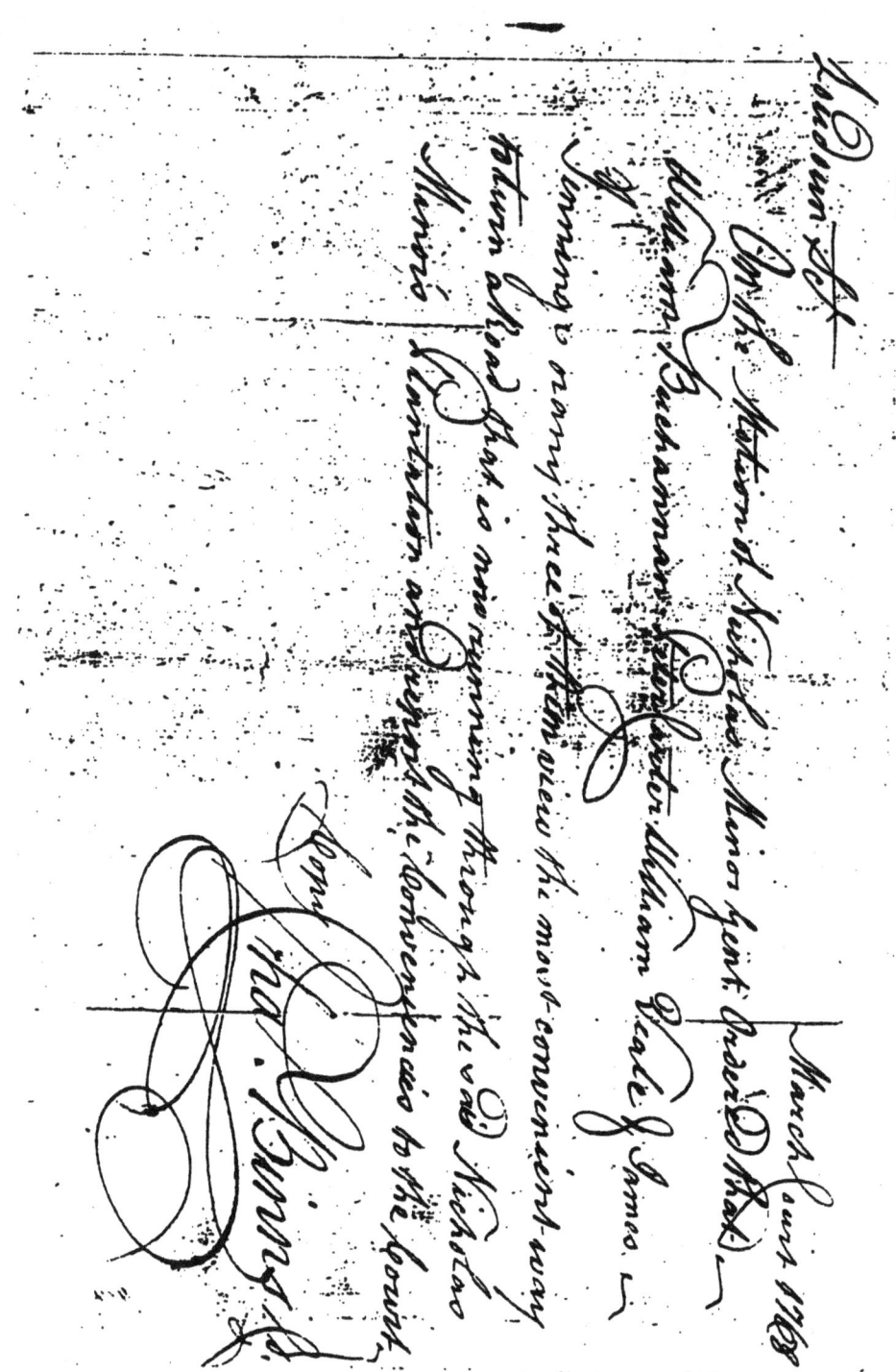

Loudoun Act

March Court 1769

On the Motion of Nicholas Minor Gent Ordered that William Buchannan Gent Surveyor William Peale & James Jennings or any three of them view the most convenient way to turn a Road that is now running through the said Nicholas Minor's Plantation and report the Inconveniences to the Court

Teste
Cha[s]. Binns [?]

March the 14 Day 1768

To the Court now sitting in Leesburgh Greeting.
The Great Road some time ago laid out from Frail Pains
Ferry to Mahlon Janney's Mill, goes through the Plantation
of your Petitioner, by which means it is very much hurt,
therefore your humble Petitioner requests liberty to move
the said Road which will be no disadvantage to the
inhabitants using the same, as it will run through more
firmer ground.

  from your Petitioner

      Edward Wyatt

William Smith
Richard Reynolds
Joseph Hils
Thomas Stump
John Stump
John Booth
Zacariah Gurly
Robert Roberson
William Dehaven
Alexis Jackson
Edmund Manning
Jacob Jones

(over)

Edward Wyatt's
Petition

Road Case File # 40 1768
Loudoun County Circuit Court
Leesburg, Virginia

March the 14 Day 1768

To the Court now sitting in Leesburgh Greeting. The Great Road some time ago Laid out from Isail Pains Ferry to Mahlon Janneys Mill, goes through the Plantation of your Petitioner, by which means it is very much hurt, therefore your Humble Petitioner Requests liberty to move the said Road which will be no Disadvantage to the Inhabitats using the same, as it will run through more firmer Ground

from your Petitioner

Edward Wyatt

William Smith
Richard Heywood
Jasper Hils
Thomas Stump
John Stump
John Boath
Zacariah Cairey
Robert Robertson
William Gehaven
Alexis Jackson
Edmund Morning
Jocob Jones

Loudoun County Court March the 15th 1768

The Petition of sundry the inhabitants, being presented and read, it is Ordered that Thomas Lewis Gent., Francis Elgin, Benjamin Shreive, and Isaac Fouch or any three of them, first being sworn before some Justice of the Peace for this County. View the most convenient way for a Road leading from Trenary's Run to William Mead's and make their Report thereof to the Court the conveniency and inconveniencies that may attend the same.

        Test.
          Cha. Binns Cl Cur

(over)

Road to be Viewed from
Trenary's Run to Mead's
by Lewis & c

Loudoun Sct
 Frans Elgin, Benjn
Shreeve & Isaac Fouch Sworn
the 4th of April, 1768 before
   Thos Lewis

Road Case File # 40　1768
Loudoun County Circuit Court
Leesburg, Virginia

Loudoun County Court, March the 15th 1768.

The Petition of sundry the Inhabitants being presented and read, It is Ordered that Thomas Lewis, Francis Elgin, Benjamin Rozzel, and Isaac South, or any three of them, being sworn before any Justice of the peace for this county, do view the most convenient way for a Road leading from Key's Ferry up to Vestal's Gap, and make report thereof to the court, the conveniencies and inconveniences the same may occasion the same.

Teste, Cha Binns Clk

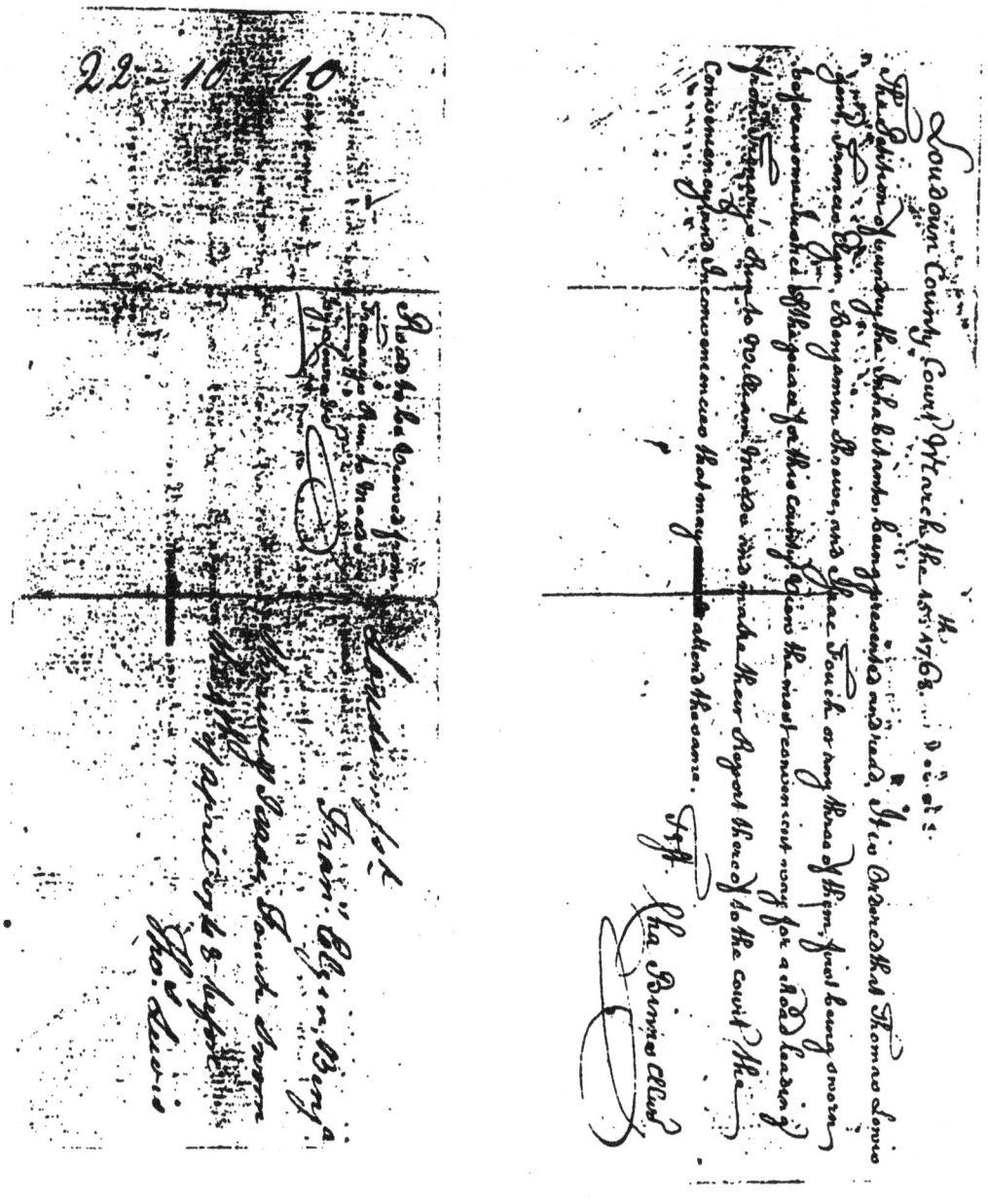

22 — 10 — 10

Loudoun Set
Francis Elgin Benj'a
Rozzel Isaac South sworn
Tho Lewis

We the Subscribers being first Sworn in obedience to an Order of Court to us directed have viewed the Road from the Road that leads to Pains Ferry and the Road at Edwart Wiet Plantation will be nearer and better to go by his House than where it is now the Road to turn off at David Muls down Jacob Shoomakers Lane to Abel Jeneys Road and from their down to Danil Lovet Plantation and to be cleared close to the fence until it comes to Georg Nixon Lane and-a between him and Shaver and from thence as the Road is now to Isral Thomsons Mill given under our hands this 9 day of April 1768.

        Samuel Gregg
        Wm Hanks
        John M^{c}ilheney

(over)

 April Court 1768
Road from Pains Ferry

April 1767 Established & William Hanks Surveyor, Jno Mucelhaney Gent. to allot the hands

Road Case File # 40 1768
Loudoun County Circuit Court
Leesburg, Virginia

We the Subscribers being first sworn in order to view
a part to es Desected to view the Road from the
head that Lead to hains george on the Rev Edwards
Plantation will be nier an Easter go by hit hither-
it is now the Road to turn of at David mils Down
Jacob Neoremakers Lane to Label Gergs Road and from
their Down to Daniel Touch plantation and to the Eease
their persecontil it Comes to george Nabeon Lane—
Cost to the persecontil it Comes from their as the
anese between him and frailer and givs in war ouse
Road is now to Is al themselves milt given in war ouse
hands this 9 day of April 1756

Samuel Gregg
D Harris
John m'Ilhany

Pursuant to the Order of Court We the Subscribers have
Viewed the Road Petitioned by Nicholas Minor Gent to have
turned from his Plantation & think that a very good Road
may be got to take it out of the old Ox Road-by-the-so along
the Mill Road to the foot of the White Ridge & so into the s'd
Ox Road opposite or just below Richard Piles's Plantation.

        William Buchener
        Peter Carter
        W'm Veale

(over)

April c'urt 1768
Report of Road
Nich Minor Gent.
April 11th O. to be cleared William
Buchener Overseer & Geo. West Gt
to allot the hands

Road Case File # 40   1768
Loudoun County Circuit Court
Leesburg, Virginia

Pursuant to the Order of Court the subscribers have
viewed the Road petitioned for by Adam Good & have
laid out a Road which we think with a little
may be got & that it will supply the Neighbourhood
the petitioners & the publick the other Road forsaid that
he now appears or is laid over Richard Peters Plantation

William Buckanan
Peter Gorts
W͟m Reade

By virtue of and in obedience to an Order of the
Worhipful the Court of Loudoun County we the
subscribers being first sworn have viewed the
way for the road in the s^d Order contain'd and
are of opinion the said Road shall be taken from
the old Road at the upper end of an old field
near the Plantation of Leven Powells running thence
along the s^d Powell & Elijah Chinns Line 'till it
comes within view of Christ^r Chinns Plantation thence
down a small Branch & crossing the same some distance
below, keeping partly a direct course to the old Road
about half a mile above the Plantation of Thomas
Chinns near where a small Path goes into the same &
that the said Road will be a more convenient way than
where it stands at present & being nearly of equal
distance as we can adjudge Witness our hands this
9th day of April 1768.

        Jonathan Tole
        John Burck
        James Battson

(over)

  April 1768
Report of a Road
  per
 Mr Thos Chinn

 April 11, 68, O. be cleared
& Thos Chinn app^d Surveyor

Road Case File # 40 1768
Loudoun County Circuit Court
Leesburg, Virginia

By Virtue and in obedience to an Order of His Worshipfull the Court of Pittsylvania County we the Subscribers being Sworn Freemen have viewed the way for the road in this Order Contained and our opinion the said Road shall be taken from the old Road at the upper end of Sr. Hubords near the Plantation of Devereaux running thence all by this Hobbsville a Chinos line till it comes within view of Hunts Chinos Plantation thence down a small branch of Sugartree Chinos Plantations boundary keeping partly a direct course to the old road about half a mile above this Plantation of Thomas Chinos Plantation and half goes into the same of that the said road will be a more convenient way than where the old Road now goes as nearly of equal distance as we can adjudge with as it being this 9th day of April 1768.

Jonathan Pole
James Bourn
James Batton

Pursuant to an Order of Court us directed bearing date, the 15th of March 1768.

We the Subscribers (three of which being first Sworn) have Viewed the most convenient way for a Road from Trenarys Run to Wm Meads, & Report as followeth (Viz) from Trenarys Run keeping the old Path through a corner of s^d Trenarys Fence to Jonathan Monkhou__ Corner Tree, & moving a few panels of said Monkhouses Fence, which appears to us to be lately made for no other use but to stop the way, thence leaving the old Path to the left hand keeping under the foot of the Mountain to (or near a Spring), thence a straight course to the old Path again where Moses Rhodes's Path comes in, thence with or near the old Path to a Branch at the corner of William Meads Meadow, thence leaving the old Path to the right hand keeping on a Ridge & falling into the Main Road ab^t 60 or 70 paces above the upper corner of Wm Meads Meadow_____ the aforesaid Road will be very convenient to the inhabitants, 'twill be some damage to Jonathan Monkhouse, & we conceive it may be of some prejudice to Lee's burg, upon the whole, in our opinion the conveniency will much surpass the inconveniencys, Witness our hands this 11th of April 1768.

                                Thos Lewis (not Sworn)
                                Fran^s Elgin
                                Isaac Fouch   Sworn
                                Benjn Shreave

(over)

Road Inter

Mead & Monkhouse in April Court 1768 the matter was debated, and appeal granted but afterwards agreed by the Parties, & Appeal dropped

Road Case File # 40 1768
Loudoun County Circuit Court
Leesburg, Virginia

Pursuant to an order of Court us directed bearing Date; the 15th of March 1768. We the Subscribers (three of which being first sworn) have viewed the most convenient way for a road from Trenarys run to Wm Meads, & Report as followeth (VIZ) from Trenarys run keeping the old path through a corner of sd Trenarys fence to Jonathan Monkhouses corner tree, & moving a few pannels of said Monkhouses fence, which appears to us to be lately made for no other use but to stop the way; thence leaving the old path to the left hand, keeping under the foot of the mountain to (or near a spring), thence a straight course to the old path again where Moses Rhodes's path comes in, thence with & near the old path to a branch at the corner of William Meads medow; thence leaving the old path to the right hand, keeping on a ridge & falling into the main road abt 60 or 70 poles above the upper corner of Wm Meads ———— the aforesaid road will be convenient to the inhabitants, it will be some damage to Jonathan Monkhouse, & we conceive it may be of some prejudice to others; upon the whole, in our opinion the conveniency will much surpass the inconveniency s, Witness our hands this 11th of April 1768.

Wm Lewis (not sworn)

Saml Lyle

Geo. _____

Wm & Shreve

To the Worshipful the Justices of Loudoun County
The petition of John Lewis humbly showeth that your
Worships have formerly made an Order for a Road to be
Established running from Broad Run in to the Mountain
Road that leads to Colchester and running through
your Petitioner on account of the said Road running through
a piece of land which is very convenient for your Petitioner
to occupy, and as your petitioner thinks that if it is
quite contrary from your Worships desire for making any
Order that would be prejudicial to any particular man and
might otherwise as well serve the conveniency of the publick
he therefore hopes your Worships will make an Order for the
said Road to be turned through the Land of Vincent Lewis
which is signified by his signing this Petition to your
Worships and would be no ways prejudicial to the publick.

           John Lewis
           Vincent Lewis

(over)

Jno. Lewis's Pet^o per
a Road
April 13. 1768. Established

Road Case File # 40   1768
Loudoun County Circuit Court
Leesburg, Virginia

To the Worshipful the Justices of Loudoun County,

The Petition of John Lewis humbly sheweth that your Worships have formerly made an Order for a Road to be Established Running from broad Run in to the Mountain Road that leads to Colchester and running through your Petitioners Land which is now and has been very prejudicial to your Petitioner on account of the said road running through a piece of Land which is very convenient for your Petitioner to Occupy, and as your Petitioner thinks that it is quite contrary from your Worships desire for making any Order that would be prejudicial to any particular man and might otherwise as well serve the conveniency of the Publick he therefore hopes your Worships will make an order for the said Road to be turned through the Land of Vincent Lewis which will also be very agreeable to the said Vincent Lewis which is signified by his signing this Petition to your Worships and also would in noways prejudicial to the Publick

John Lewis

Vincent Lewis

Pursuant to an Order of Court to us directed
We the Subscribers being first qualified thereto
carefully Viewed the way from John Ozbourns to the
William's Gap Road, and are of opinion that the most
convenient way (the people being generally satisfied
therewith) may be beginning at said Ozbourns House,
and from thence as we have Marked passing near Richard
Ozbourns Philip Slaughs and so into the above said
Gap Road.

November 8th, 1768_____   Joshua Gore
                                 Francis Ferguson

(over)

Gore & Fergusons
Report of a Road

November 14, 1768, Ordered to
be opened pursuant to Report &
Thomas Humphreys Overseer
Fr^s. Peyton G^t. to allot the hands

Road Case File # 40   1768
Loudoun County Circuit Court
Leesburg, Virginia

Pursuant to an Order of Court to us directed We the Subscribers being first Satisfied Thereto Carefully Viewed the Way from John Osbourns to William's Gap Road and are of Opinion that a most Convenient way (the public being Generally Satisfied therewith) may be beginning at said Osbourns Gate, and from thence as will Marked, Makeing Near Richard Osbourns Philip Slaughs and so into the above said Gap Road

November 7th 1766

Joshua Gore
Thomas [Ferguson?]

Miscellaneous Road Cases File No. 41, 1769
Clerk of Circuit Court
Archives
Leesburg, Virginia

Loudoun County Court   November the 15th 1768

Upon the Petition of James Stephens and sundry others, for a Road to be opened to the Town and Courthouse from John Lewis's and said Stephens's into an old Road leading over the Mountain, It is Ordered that Craven Peyton and Stephen Donaldson Gent. and William Baker or any two of them being first sworn View the way Petitioned for and Report to the Court the conveniencies and inconveniencies that may attend the public in opening and clearing the same.

Stephen Donaldson Gent. & Wm Baker   Test
Sworn before me.
                        Cha' Binns Cl cur
         Craven

(over)

Peyton & others
to View a Road
April 10   Established

Pursuant to the within Order of Court, we the Subscribers being first qualified as within directed have View'd the way Petitioned for and Report, that a Road may be had along the said way, to suit the Petitioners, without inconvenience to the publick, or prejudice to any private person, as the Road intended will direct it's course from the Plantation of Old Abbett along near a Plantation of Philip Saunders's, and through a Lane of John Lewis's, and from thence through this Land of Thompson Mason Esqr near a Plantation of his, call'd Rasberry Plane, and through a piece of low ground near the foot of the Mountain, and into the old Road within mention'd, and across the same about 4 or 5 hundred yards to the Plantation of the within nam'd James Stephens.

                            Stephen Donaldson
                            Wm Baker

Road Case File # 41   1769
Loudoun County Circuit Court
Leesburg, Virginia

Loudoun County Court November the 15th 1768.

"Upon the Petition of James Stephens and sundry others, for a Road to be opened to the Town and Court house from John Lewis's and said Stephens's into an old road leading over the mountain. It is Ordered that Craven Peyton and Stephen Donaldson Gent and William Baker or any two of them being first sworn View the way Petitioned for and Report to the Court the Conveniencies and Inconveniencies that may attend the Public in Opening and clearing the same.

Test Cha' Binns Clk"

Peyton & others
to View a Road
April 10th 1768 [?]

"Pursuant to the within Order of Court, we the Subscribers being first qualified as within directed have View'd the way Petitioned for and Report, that a Road may be had along the said way, to suit the Petitioners without Inconvenience to the Publick, or Prejudice to any private Person; as the Road intended will direct it's course from the Plantation of Old Mr Abbott along near a Plantation of Philip Saunders's, and through a Lane of [...] from thence through the Land of Thompson Mason Esqr. near [...] this call'd Newberry Lane, and through a piece of low-ground near the [...] into the Old Road within mention'd, and across the same about [...] yards to the Plantation of the within Named James Stephens—

Stephen Donaldson
Wm Baker"

1767

Agreeable to an Order from Loudoun County Court we do agree that from the Forks of the Leesburg & Winchester Road that the most convenient way to Bull Run is for the Road to go by where Charles West now lives & from thence to the new Road now cleared & so along the said new Road to Bull Run Given under our hands this 20 day of March 1769.

       John Davis (Surveyor)
       Henry Ringo
       John Smarr
       ~~Samuel Wyckoff~~
       John Hall

(over)

The Viewers
Report

April 10 Established accordg
to Report and Davis Surveyor
Contd

Road Case File #41   1769
Loudoun County Circuit Court
Leesburg, Virginia

Agreeable to an Order from Governor Gooch Survey'd for Joseph Lane that Parcel of the fork of the Licking being part of a greater Tract the most convenient way to agree with the lines laid down for that by other orders now Survey'd for Richard Randolph to run to the N.E. to go Nine Mountains So along the various courses to Hickman run sixteen Chains then N. 20 deg. W. 73 Poll.

John Ornis (Surveyor)
Thomas Ringo
John Lanier
Lawrence Hughes
John Hall

Loudoun County Sct.   March Court   1769

   Ordered that Isaac Nichols Jr., Joshua Gore, Thomas
Gore & Benjamin Pool or any three of them being first
sworn before a Justice of this County do view the most
convenient way for a Road to be turned near Samuel
Smith's and make a Report of the conveniency and
inconveniency that may attend the same to the Court.

                         Copy
                            Cha. Binns Cl.

(over)

Nichols Isaac & Gore
to View a Road

1769 April 10 Rept. Retd.
and Road established
accordingly

Road Case File # 41 1769
Loudoun County Circuit Court
Leesburg, Virginia

Loudoun County ss.   April Court 1769.

Ordered that for a View to be had of the nearest and best way from Charles Bennett's through the Gap in the Short Hill to the County line near Key's Ferry, that Thomas Lewis, Francis Hague, Isaac Hollingsworth, and Thomas Shore, or any three of them, do view the most convenient way for the said road, and make a Report of the conveniency and inconveniency that may attend the same to this Court —

Copy   [signature]

Pursuant and in obedience to an Order of Loudoun County Court to us directed we the subscribers having met and examined the Road as therein mentioned and Report as followeth that the Road laid out and cleared by Samuel Smith is equal to or better than any place it can be made but is about twenty four yards further than the place marked formerly and the conveniency that attends the keeping it as it now stands is that it runs nearly as the dividing line between the s^d Smith & Joseph Richardson and leaves clear about three acres of high land and about one and a half acres of meadow land which the other Road would make of little or no use to the said Smith ___
Given under our hands this 10th day of April 1769.

           Thos Gore
           Isaac Nichols
           Joshua Gore
           Benjamin Pool

Road Case File # 41   1769
Loudoun County Circuit Court
Leesburg, Virginia

Pursuant and [conditional?] to an Order of Loudoun Co[unty]
Court to us [Directed?] the Subscribers having met and
examined the [Road?] therein mentioned and Repo[rt]
as followeth that the Road laid out and cleared by [said?]
Smith is equal [or?] better than any place it can be [made?]
but is about Twenty four yards further than the place
mark'd formerly and the Conveniency that attends the
keeping it as it now stands is that it Runs nearly as
the Dividing Line Between the sd Smith & Joseph
Richardson and Leaves clear about three acres of high
Land and about two and an half acres of meadow land
which the other Road would make of little or no use
to the said Smith Given under our hands this 10th day
of april 1769.

Thos Gore
Isaac Nickols
Joshua Gore
Benjamin [Jay?]

In pursuance & obedience to an Order of the Worshipful Court of Loudoun County to view a Road Petitioned for by James Leith, we the Subscribers being first sworn are of opinion the s^d Leith should have liberty to open the same & that the said Road shall go on the upper side of the s^d Taylors Field & then the straightest way to the House of the s^d Taylors & from thence to go thro^t the Plantation to a large Gate made use of by the s^d Taylor to go to market & that the s^d Leith have liberty to fix a Gate or a p^t of bars where a little Gate now stands leading out of the s^d Taylors Pasture for a way to Mill, provided never the less if the s^d Henry Taylor will make sufficient a small part of the Road which he has clear'd to the Mill that is to say, to cut down a hillside just opposite his Still-house so as to make the same passable that the s^d Leith shall not have liberty to go tho^t the Plantation in his way to Mill Under our hands this 10th April 1769.

        Leven Powell
        Elijah Chinn

(over)

Powell & Chinn's Report of
Ja^s Leith's Road

10 April 1769 Rep^t returned
and Road established accordingly

Leith James   Road

Road Case File # 41   1769
Loudoun County Circuit Court
Leesburg, Virginia

In pursuance of obedience to an order of the worshipful Court of Loudoun County to review a road petitioned for by James Leith, we the subscribers being first sworn are of opinion Mr.d Leith should have liberty to open the same & that the said Road shall go on the upper side of Mr.d Taylors field & then the straitest way to the house of Mr.d Taylors house & from thence to go thro. the plantation to a large gate made use of by Mr.d Taylor to go to market & that Mr.d Leith have liberty to fix a gate or a pr. of Barrs where a little gate now stands leading out of Mr.d Taylors pasture for a way to mill. Provided nevertheless if Mr.d Henry Taylor will make sufficient a small part of the road which he has cleard to the mill that is to say, to cut down a hill side just opposite his still house so as to make the same passable that Mr.d Leith shall not have liberty to go thro. the plantation in his way to — Given our hands this 10th April 69.

Leven Powell
Elijah Chinn

Pursuant to an Order of Loudoun County Court we the subscribers being first sworn have Viewed the most convenient way from the Meetinghouse as in the s^d Order is directed across the Mountain to Mr. Thompson Masons Mill and find a convenient Road may be had withour prejudice to any person (which way for the s^d Road to be laid off we have marked) 13th April 1769

                                his
                         John X Cavins
                            mark
                         John Best
                         James Ratekin

(over)

Road
Cavens & others Report of a Road

April 13th 1769 Ret^d & Established
John Cavens app^d Surveyor, and
James Hamilton G^t to allot the hands

Road Case File # 41 1769
Loudoun County Circuit Court
Leesburg, Virginia

Pursuant to an order of Loudoun County Court for
the or[d]ering a Convenient road or roads leading over
the most convenient way from the Midway
house as in the Ord. order so directed across the
Mountain to Mr. Thompson Mefaras Mill and
find a Convenient road may be had without
any considerable prejudice to any person, so hath we had that
prejudice to the laid off we have marks
Road the laid off we have marks
18 August 1769

John K Carter
his
John Boyh
James Watkins

To the Honourable Court of Loudoun

We your Petitioners humbly showeth, that whereas there hath been a Road leading through our neighborhood upwards of twenty years that some of us do certainly know of; and continues to be a Road much used, espcially to Israel Thompson's Mill & c__ but as there never hath been an Order of Court to Establish & Confirm the same; some men have turned the Road so out of the old & best way that it is almost impracticable to pass, especially with carriages. Therefore we hope you will please to allow us a Road beginning at a convenient part of the Road; leading from the Mountain (by the Baptist Meeting House) to Leesburg; and from thence through Joshua Gore's Lane, directly with, or near the old way, passing through John Bonds, Robert Todds & Thomas Townsends Lots; and so to the above said Thompson's Mill, &, C__ ____ and we your Petitioners shall ever pray._____

Thomas Humphrey
Timothy Hixson
George Lewis
John Marks
Phillip Slaught
John Whittcre
Samuel Compton
Nicolus Osbirn
John Brown
James Nichols

John Pierce
Stephen Lewis
Philip Hoff
John Willson
Richard Thacher
Henry Ferguson

(over)

Petition for a Road

13 April 1769 O^d that Jos^a Gore Saml Compton, Thos Pursley, and Benj^a Burson or any three being sworn View the way Pet^d for and report to the Cur. & c.

Road Case File # 41   1769
Loudoun County Circuit Court
Leesburg, Virginia

To the Honourable Court of Loudoun

We Your Petitioners Humbly Sheweth, That whereas there hath been a Road Leading through Our Neighbourhood upwards of Twenty Years that some of us do Certainly know of; and Continues to be a Road much Used, Especially to Israel Thompson's Mill &c — but as there never hath been an Order of Court to Establish & Confirm the same; some Men have turned the road so out of the Old & best way That it is Almost Impracticable to pass, Especially with Carriages. — Therefore we hope you will please to allow us a Road Begining at a Convenient part of the Road, Leading from the Mountain (by the Baptist Meeting House) to Leesburg; and from thence through Joshua Gore's Lane, Directly with, or Near the Old way, passing through John Bond's, Robert Todd & Thomas Townsend's Lotts; and So to the above said Thompson's Mill &c — and we Your Petitioners Shall ever Pray —

Thomas Humphrey
Timothy Hixson
George Lewis
John Charles
Phillip Slaught
John Kilmore
Samuel Compton
Nicolus Osburn
John Brown
James Nichols

John Pearce
Stephen Lewis
Phillip Hoff
John Willson
Richert Thacker
Henry Ferguson

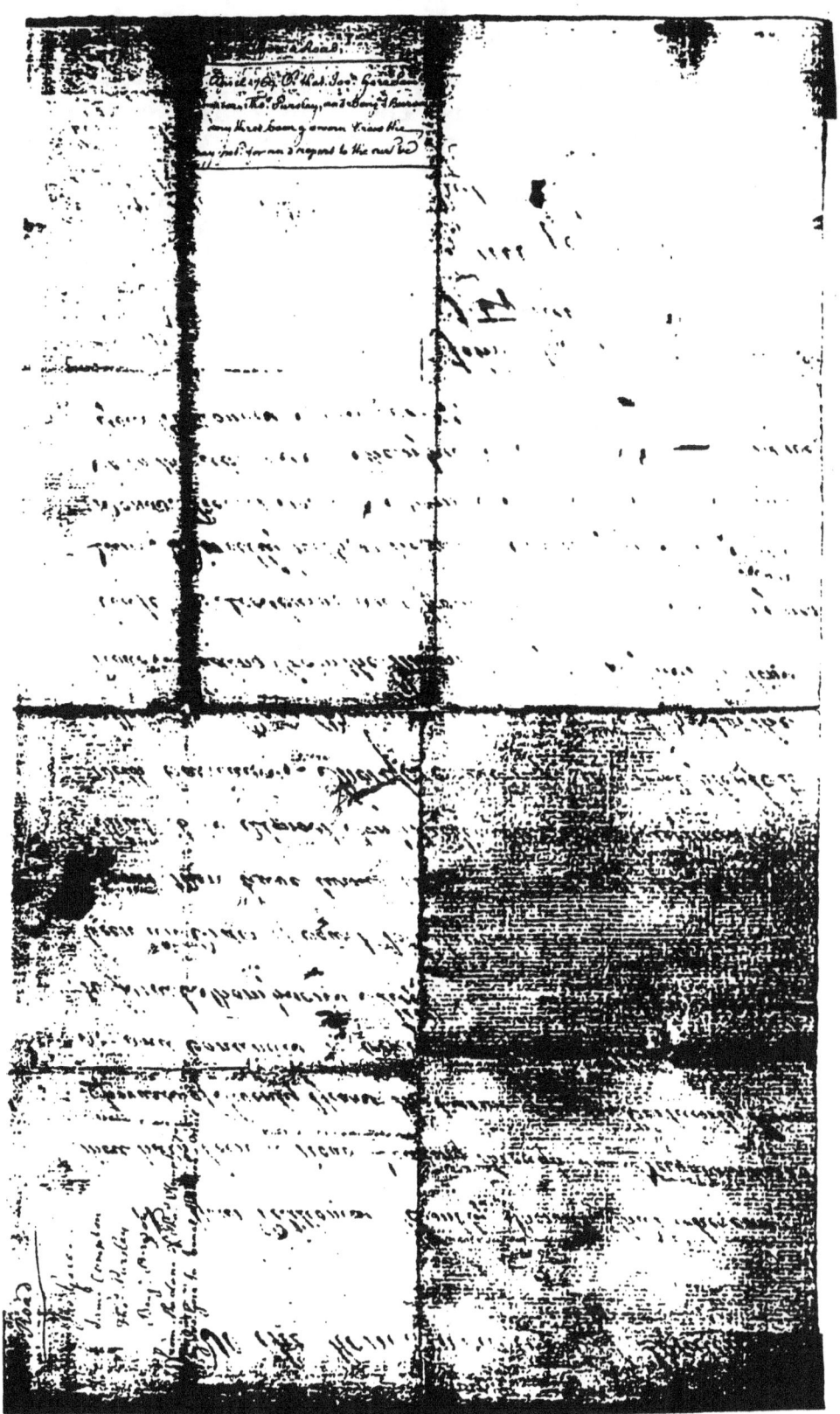

Loudoun County Court   August the 14th, 1769

Upon a Petition of sundry of the inhabitants praying for a Road to be cleared from the Road that leads to Snigger's Gap, by John Pearce's, and to take out near the said Pearce's and from thence to cross the Road that leads from Leesburg to Snigger's Gap, about four miles from the Ridge, and from thence the nearest and best way to Isaac Nickol's Mill and into the same Road near Jacob Janneys Mill, as they think it would answer to better purpose than where it now is. It is Ordered that William Janney, William Brown, Samuel Compton and Joshua Gore or any three of them being first sworn before a Justice of the Peace View the way so as aforesaid Petitioned for and Report to the Court whether it may be convenient for the publick to have the same opened.

a Copy Cha' Binns Cl Court

(over)
Janney William & others
to View a Road

We the subscribers having View'd the way as within directed, find that there may be a Road had to suit the convenience of the Petitioners without prejudice to any private person. Certify under our hands this 9th of Oct.r 1769

Samuel Compton
W.m Janney
Will.m Brown

W.m Janney and William Brown were qualified before

Ja.s Hamilton
2'd Oct.r 1769

Samuel Compton was this day sworn to Report to the Court of Loudoun County as the within Order of Court directs, to the best of his knowledge. Certified under my hand this 9th day of Oct.r 1769

1769 Octo' 11, Established according to Report, & John Warfurd app.d Surveyor, Ja.s Hamilton Gent to allot the hands

Road Case File # 41   1769
Loudoun County Circuit Court
Leesburg, Virginia

Louisa County Court August 11th 1769

Upon the petition of sundry of the Inhabitants praying for a road to be cleared from the [...] across from the [...] to [...] Read the said [...] and from thence to [...] from thence to [...] Niggers Gap, about four miles from the Ridge, and from thence the nearest & best way to Joseph Nichols's Mill [...] to appear Jacob Arnold, Smith [...] Kings [...] and wherever it may run, It is Ordered that Wm. Johnson, Charles Copeland, John Gore or any three of them being first sworn before a Justice & [...] the same, the way so as aforesaid petitioned for and report to the Court where they may be convenient for the Public to have the same opened.

Copy Cha: Barrett Clk

Miscellaneous Road Cases File No. 42, 1770
Clerk of Circuit Court
Archives
Leesburg, Virginia

Loudoun County Court   August the 13th 1770

Upon a Petition of Sundry Inhabitants for a Road from the Loudoun Line into the Great Mountain Road that leads from West's Ordinary to Snicker's, it is Ordered that, Jacob Reed, John Smarr, John Stall and Sylvester Gardner, or any three of them being first sworn before a Justice of the Peace View the way Petitioned for, and Report to the Court whether it may be convenient to the public to have the same opened.

                            Test
                              Cha's Binns Cl Cur

(over)

Order for a Road

Loudoun County Sep'r August the 18th 1770 —

Upon a Petition of sundry Inhabitants for a Road from the Loudoun Line into "the great mountain Road that leads from Wools ordinary to Snickers"

It is Ordered that Jacob Reed John Jenner, John Stak and Cheveler Gardner, or any three of them being first sworn before a Justice of the peace Doe View the way Petitioned for, and Report to the Court whether it may be convenient to the publick to have the same opened.

Teste Chas Binns Cl.

To the Worshipful Court of Loudoun County Greeting
Whereas we the humble Petitioners desire that as
there is an Order of Court for a Road to the Mouth
of Catoctan passed for the benefit of Wm Aubery
and as the Road is not beneficial to the inhabitants
of them parts and shall be at great cost for the
clearing of the same hoping that your Worships will
take it into your consideration and relieve us from
the great expense that we shall be obliged to bear
on the same as the s^d Aubery is not able to perform
the keeping of the Ferry according to what he has
performed and as the Road is to go from the Mouth of
Catoctan to Wm Kirks Mill as it is very prejudicial
to the inhabitants of these parts as it is well known
and we whose names are under written can certify the
same as it can be made to appear for which we the
humble Petitioners shall pray & c^o

(underwritten by 38 freeholders by their signatures)

(over)

Pet^o for Road
Sep^t 11, 1770   Read & Ordered that the
s^d Road ment^d in the Pet^o desist in
having the same cleared until
Thos Awbrey prepares a proper boat
for the Ferry and until the further
Order of this Court

Ordered that the Overseer of this Road let it lye
uncleared til Awbrey has a proper Boat & a Road
in Maryland

Road Case File # 42   1770
Loudoun County Circuit Court
Leesburg, Virginia

To the Worshipful Cort of Loudoun County
Greeting whereas we the humble petitioners Desire that
whereas there is an order of Cort for a road to the mouth
of Cotetin past for the Benefit of Wm Hickery and as the
Road is not Benificial to the inhabitants of these parts
and Shall be at a great Cost for the Clearing of
the same hoping that your Worships will take
it into your Consideration and Relieve us from
the great Expence that we shall be obliged to
be hear on the same as the sd Hickery is not able
to perform the thegoing of the forsy ther ding to
What he he has performed and as the Road is to go
from the mouth of Cotetin to Wm Hortons Mill
as it is very Prejudicial of to the inhabitants of these
parts as it is well known and we whose Names are
underwritten Can Certify the same as it can be made
appear for which we the Humble petitioners
Shall pray &c Erasmus Gadneich

John Dell
James Wanseal X
Edward Johns
ad wanseal

John Sutton
Jacob Gramour
 Will

Robert [illegible]
[illegible]
Johann [illegible]
[illegible]
Wm [illegible]
Peter [illegible]
[illegible]
Daniel Bell
Jacob [illegible]
[illegible]
Johann [illegible]
[illegible]
Math [illegible]
[illegible]
[illegible]
[illegible]
Charles Seaton

To the Worshipful Court of Loudoun C^y
The Petition of John & James Steer humbly shoveth
that there has been a View for a Road to be cleared
from William Kirks Mill through their Land w^c is
highly prejudicial to them and also about &
inconvenient to the publick as the Report was
Returned. Your Petitioners therefore Pray the said
Road may be Reviewed.

(over)

Petition for a Road
from Kirks Mill
to be Reviewed

Road Case File # 42   1770
Loudoun County Circuit Court
Leesburg, Virginia

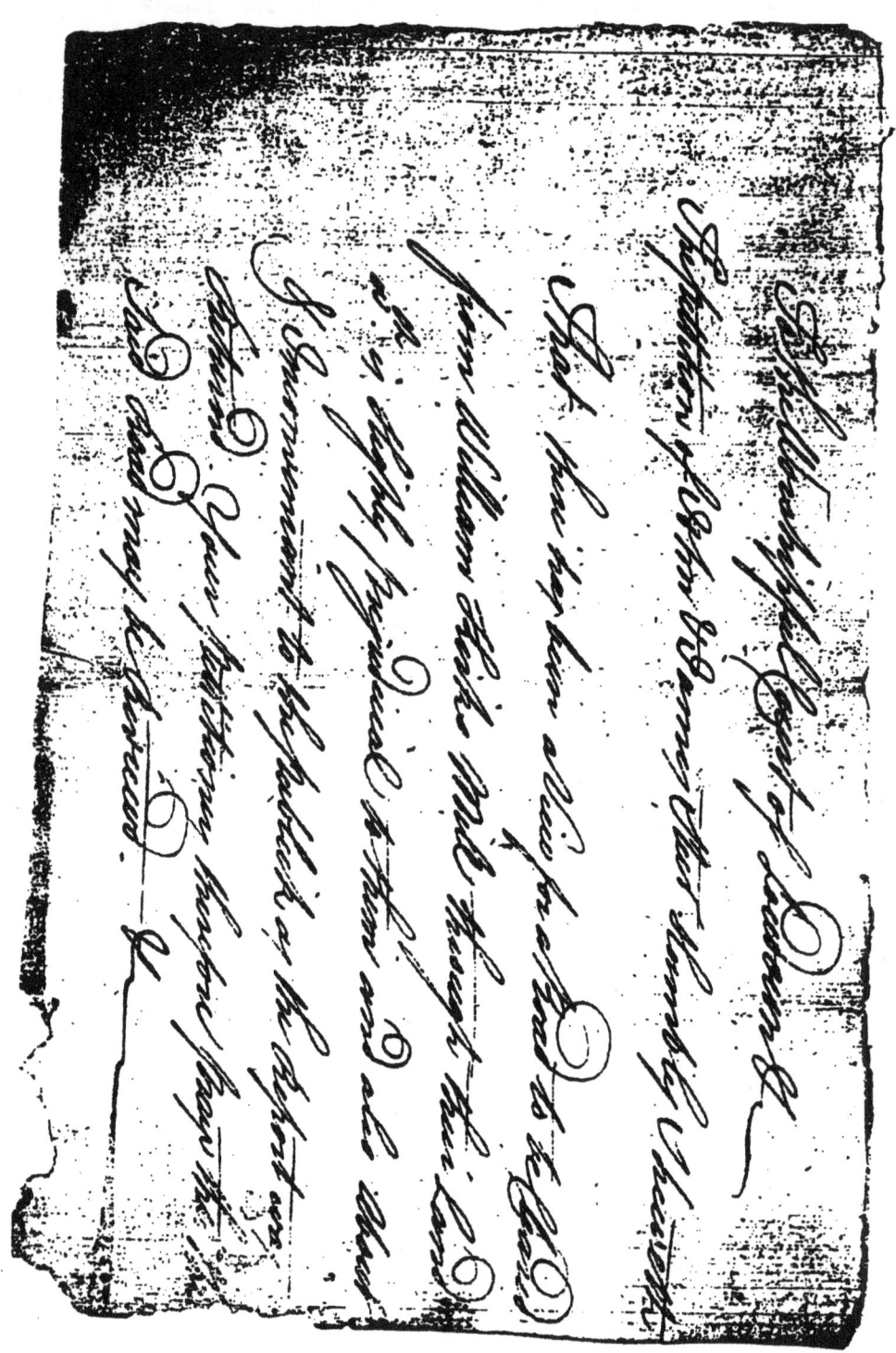

To the Worshipfull Court of Sussex &c

The Petition of John Bowne Humbly Sheweth

That there has been a Suet for a Tract to fall
from William Heck Mill though their Land
to his highest purpose to them and also there
Is Grievance to the Publick as the Report can
Show Your Petitioner humbly prays the
Said Road may be Reviewed &c

Miscellaneous Road Cases File No. 43, 1771
Clerk of Circuit Court
Archives
Leesburg, Virginia

By virtue of & in obedience to an Order of the worshipful Court of Loudoun we the Subscribers being first sworn have viewed the way as directed in the s^d Order and are of opinion that a good Road may be opened w^h we have laid off in the following manner, beginning at Fauq. County Line at the end of the new Road cleared by an Order of the Court of Fauquier & running thence to Benj^a Chandlers & thro' his Plantation as the old Road formerly went to the Corner of the Widow Morin's Field thence by James Lampkins Plantation and crossing Little River at the Mouth of Wm Berkleys Spring Branch to Powells Mill Road & with the s^d Road to Snickers Gap Road & that the same will be convenient for sundry inhabitants in the Bull Run Mountains Given under our hands this 30th March 1771.

      Jacob Reed
      John Hall
       his
     (?) X Garner
       Mark

(over)

Road Report

Report of Road from West's
Ordinary to Snicker's gap

 April 8th 1771
Established per Report and
William Berkley Overseer &
Leven Powell Gen^t to allot the
hands

Road Case File # 43 1771
Loudoun County Circuit Court
Leesburg, Virginia

April 1771 — To the worshipful Court of Loudoun the Petition of Wm Brown & Co. showeth that about twelve months ago, he & sundry's(sic) Petitioned the Court for a Road to be laid of from the Kitockton Meetinghouse by Goose Creek Meetinghouse to Isaac Nichols's Mill, & that your Worships at that time appointed Men to View the same & Report the conveniency & _ & whereas the Men then appointed never have executed the s^d Order your Petitioner pray, that other men may be appointed or such relief as in that Case your Worships shall think proper.

Wm Brown

(over)

Browns Pet^n for Road

April 9th 1771
Ordered that Owen Roberts, John Dodd, James Hamilton, and John Cavens or any three, View the way and Report the Conv^s to the Court

Road Case File # 43 1771
Loudoun County Circuit Court
Leesburg, Virginia

Middlesex ss. } County of Loudoun

To the Moderator of the Broad run Church

That whereas Epaphroditus Epps, is known as a partner for all appearance by s[ome] from the Scriptures making some by some such making some [illegible] such Rules, will - & that your Church shall some appointed Ministers & Deacons & that the commencement, witness whose hereunto are hereunto placed this Letter Your petitioner prays that this man may be admitted to such relief as his case your Worships shall think proper.

Wm Brown

To the Worshipful Court of Loudoun
The Petition of John Hough & co therewith that your
Petitioners are of opinion that the Road from
Leesburgh to Alexandria would go by Hough's Mill a
nearer & better way than it does at present & would
therefore be advantageous to the publick.- Therefore
Pray, that men may be appointed to View the same
from Leesburgh by s^d Mill & thence into the Road
leading to Broad Run Bridge & make Report to the
Court & co.

(over)

Hough & co for Road
April 10th 1771
Ordered that Wm Mead, John Lewis, Fleming Patterson
& Wm Douglass Gent or any three View the way &
Report

Order them -
Wm Mead
John Lewis
Flem^g Patterson
& Wm Douglass
or 3 of them
View & co.

Road Case File # 43 1771
Loudoun County Circuit Court
Leesburg, Virginia

Distances &c

Baltimore to Georgetown 40 Miles
(none being given from Elk Ridge)
Elk Ridge from Baltimore is about [illegible] through the
Baltimore and Frederick Road is thence from Elk ridge
to Alexandria will go by Bladensburgh the other 8 Miles
way from Bladensburgh could not be ascertained Montgomery
Court House — Snicker's Ferry that from May be
afforded to view the same from Leesburgh to U? Mill
5 mile and the Road leading to Broad run bridge
5 mile to Lands lef[t] &c

Loudoun County Court   November the 12th   1770

A Petition of sundry the inhabitants being read and considered, it is Ordered that William Brown, George Taverner, William Hatcher and Merser Brown or any three of them being first sworn or affirmed as the case may be before some Justice of the Peace of this County View the way Petitioned for from Israel Thompsons Mill to a new Mill of John Brown and others, and report to the Court whether it may be convenient to the public to have a Road opened.
       Test
        Cha's Binns Cl Cur

(over)

19th Jan.Y   1771
  the Wm brown was
  qualifd
    Jas Hamilton

In obedience to the within Order we have viewed the Road petitioned for and we are all of opinion the Road should not be opened as its a very troublesome way and of no great use.

  For
William Brown & c.
 View Road

may 13th   1771, Rejected as being unnecessary

Road Case File # 43   1771
Loudoun County Circuit Court
Leesburg, Virginia

Loudoun County Court November the 12. 1770

A Petition of sundry the Inhabitants being read and considered, It is Ordered that William Brown, George Tavenner, William Hatcher and Moses Brown or any three of them being first sworn or affirmed with the case enjoin'd be, & they are hereby appointed to view the way petition'd for in the petition of Moses Brown, Wm. Brown and others, and report to the court whether it may be convenient to the Public to have a Road opened.

Teft Cha: Binns Clk

To the Worshipful Court of Loudoun humbly complaining
showeth unto your Worships that the Mountain Road as
it now runs through your Petitioners Land is of great
prejudice and that there may be as good a way and
nearer for the s^d Road to go on the Line betwixt your
Petitioner and Jacob Ramey & Neals Heirs and y^r
Petitioner humbly Prays that y^r Worships may order a
Review and Report & shall Pray &.

       Samuel Love

(over)

Ja^s Lane, George Summers G^t, Fielding Turner
and Jeremiah Hutchison or any three.

Loves
Petition
for a Road

G. Summers
James Lane Gent.
J. Brown

Love Saml for Road
May 13th 1771 Order for View

Road Case File # 43 1771
Loudoun County Circuit Court
Leesburg, Virginia

To the Worship[ful]
Loudoun Humb[ly]
sheweth unto your [Worships that the]
Mountain Road as it now runs through
your Petitioners Lands is of Great
Prejudice and that there may be
as good a way and nearer for the Drove
to go on the Line between your Peti=
=tioner and Jacob Reamey of w[hi]ch
Herein and y[ou]r Petitioner humbly
Prays that y[ou]r Worships may order
a review and Report & shall
pray &c
                Samuel Love

Your Petitioner humbly showeth that they labour under a very great disadvantage in repairing the Road from Piney Branch to Little River by reason of the long distance being at least seven or eight miles, and is also a great inconveniency to the Surveyors of the said Road in warning so large a company to work on the Road. Therefore your Petitioners prays your Worships would divide the said Road and company distinctly from Piney Branch to Saml Wikeoffs Spring to be one District, and from the said Spring to Little River, and the hands to be allotted and your Petitioners in duty bound shall pray & ___

John Haddocks	Joseph Reeder
Garrat Snedcker	Thomas Lake
	John Huff
	Jeames Bennet
	John Downs
	George Dawdle
	Cornelius Anderson
	Samuel Wyckoff
	William Beavers
	Tunes Johnson
	Andrew Beaty
	Jeames Beaty
	William Beaty
	George Durin
Henry Ringo Lower cont^d	David Reeder
Sam1. Wyckoff	Joseph Hutchison

(over)

Petition for Road

June 10th 1771 Road divided & Saml Wycoff of the Upper part & Henry Ringo, of the Lower, and hands as per list inside

(continued on two additional sheets of paper as follows)

Road Case File # 43 1771
Loudoun County Circuit Court
Leesburg, Virginia

Note: Apparently, the Piney Branch of Beaverdam Creek in southwestern Loudoun County, Virginia.

To the Worshipfull Court of Loudoun County

Your petitioners Humbly Sheweth that they labour under a very great Disadvantage in repairing the Road from Piney Branch to Little River by reason of the long distance being at least Seven or eight Miles, and is also a great Inconveniency to the Surveyors of the said road in warning so large a company to work on the road. Wherefore your petitioners prays your worships would divide the said Road and Company distinctly from Piney Branch to Sam.l Wikoff's spring to be one District, and from the said spring to Little river, and the hands to be allotted and your petitioners in duty bound shall ever pray &c.

John Maddocks
Gavrat Sneedeker

Henry Rings Lower Cart.d
Sand Veyor of road

Joseph R___
Thomas Like
John ____

Jeames Bennet
John Downs
George Dowdle
Cornelius Anderson
Samuel Wykoff
William Bravers
Shines Johnson
Thomas ____
Andrew beaty
Jas m. beaty
William beaty
George Dunn
David Reeder
Joseph Hutchison

(sheet A)

Henry Ringo Surveyor	2 Hands
Joseph Hutchison	2
John Huff	1
Willm Waldin	2
John Hadocks	2
John Waldin	4
George Deurin	2
Joseph Reedor	2
Thos Lake	1
Daniel Reedor	1
David Reedor	1

The Hands to be allotted to the Lower part of the Road.

(sheet B)

Garret Snedcker	1
Thomas West	4
Robert Beaty	3
Saml Wyckoff	2
Tunes Johnson	2
George Dawdle	1
Cornelius Anderson	2
Jeames Hoker	1
William Beavers	1
Jeames Bennet	1
John Downs	1

The above Hands to be allotted to the Upper part of the Road under Saml Wycoff Overseer

Road Case File # 43   1771
Loudoun County Circuit Court
Leesburg, Virginia

Henry Ringo Servant 2 Hands	
Joseph Hutcheson — 2	Garret Parker — 1
John Huff —	Thomas West —
Will'm Huff — 1	Robart Beaty — 1
John Waklin — 2	Sam'l Wright — 3
John Hagocks — 2	James Wright — 2
George Dewyn — 4	George Davidson —
John Waklin —	James Johnson — 2
Joseph Agnor — 2	Cornelis Anderson — 2
Tho.s Lake — 1	James Hoker — 1
James Agnor — 1	William Beavers — 1
Dav.d Agnor — 1	James Bennah — 1
their hands to be allotted to the home	John Downs — 1
at of the home	Their hands to be allotted to the upper fifty hund under Cam Wyoch avenue

98

Loudoun County Court   November the 12th 1770

A Petition of sundry inhabitants being read praying a Road from Richard Thatchers in Williams Gap to Shepard Mill and from thence into the Main Road leading to Leesburg being considered It is Ordered that Thomas Pursley, Joshua Gore, Robert Jamieson, and Nicholas Osborn or any three of them being first sworn or affirmed as the case may be, before some Justice of the Peace of this County View the way Petitioned for and report to the Court whether it may be convenient to the public to have a Road opened.

                Test   Cha's Binns Cl Cur

(over)

For
Thomas Pursley & c.
View Road

Loudoun Sct

      Agreeable to the within Order Thomas Pursley, Joshua gore & Robt Jamison was Sworn before me this 10th day of August 1771   Certified under my hand

                Flemming Patterson

Road Case File # 43   1771
Loudoun County Circuit Court
Leesburg, Virginia

Loudoun County Court November the 12. 1770

A Petition of sundry the Inhabitants being read and considered, it is Ordered that William Brown, George Favener, William Hatcher and Thomas Brown or any three of them being first sworn or affirmed as the case may be before some Justice of Peace of this County View the way between for of on Lot and Thomas Smith to a new Mill of John Brown and others, and report to the court whether it may be convenient to the Public to have a Road opened

Tes[t]: Chas Binns [Clk]

Loudoun County Court, May the 13th 1771

Upon the Petition of Samuel Potts and others praying for a Road to be opened from Pott's Mill across the Hon'ble George William Fairfax's Land into the Main Road leading to Vestals Gap, also from the said Mill along under the Blue Ridge to the end of John Osborn Senr his line. It is Ordered that, Joshua Gore, Robert Jamieson, and Benjamin Huff, first being duly sworn, do View the way Petitioned for and Report to the Court upon Oath the conveniencies or inconveniencies that may attend such Roads being opened.

      Test Cha's Binns Cl Cur

(over)

Potts Samuel
Road to be Viewed

June 11th 1771
Robert Jamison & Benjn Hough
Sworn before me.
    J. Clapham

Road Case File # 43 1771
Loudoun County Circuit Court
Leesburg, Virginia

Loudoun County Court May the 10, 1774

Upon a Petition of Samuel Potts and others praying for a Road to be opened from Potts Mill a nearer the Humble George Road, then runs from Leesburg near the Mountains Road leading to Goose along from the said Smith under the Blue Ridge to the Gap of John Osborn above his Line, This Ordered that Joshua George, Abraham Davisson, and Benjamin Hough, first being duly sworn, do View the way they propose for and Report to the Court upon Oath the Conveniences or Inconveniences that may attend such Road being opened.

Teste Cha. Binns Clk

In obedience to an Order of May Term 1771-
for a Road from Potts Mill across the Honorable George
Wm Fairfax's Land into the Main Road leading over at Vestal
Gap and we do allow and Report as follows viz. through
Ezeikle Potts land thence through David Williams Land and
John Rusel Land thence near the line of said Williams
and said Rusels line thence through a corner of John
Aruecosts Land thence through Even Evens Land thence
through Valintine Millers and on or near the line betwixt
said Miller and John Perces Land thence through Henry
Michel Land into the Main Road leading to said Gap against
the Road that leads Betwixt the Hills to Robt. Harpers
Ferry, also from the said Mill across the said Ezekiel
Potts Land and on or near the line betwixt said Potts and
David Williams near to the Mill Pond thence through said
Ezekiel Potts Land thence through Nathan Potts Land thence
through Thomas Pursleys Land thence through Thomas Levelion
Land to John Osborn Senior Fence twenty poles above the
said Lane thence down said Osborn Fence to the end of said
Lane which we Return as a Publick Road to your Worships:
As Witness our hands.

September 7th 1771-   Robt Jamison
                                   Benjamin Hoff

(over)

A Return of a Road
from and to Potts
Mill for Septm
Term 1771

    No 1
1771 Sept. 9 Ordered that Jos. Gore,
Henry Smith, Simon Mathews and
John Osborn or any three upon Oath
View the former way Petd for from
Potts Mill to Vestals Gap & report

Road Case File # 43   1771
Loudoun County Circuit Court
Leesburg, Virginia

In obedience to a order of a may Sion 1774
for a Road from Potts mill across the honrable George Wm Fairfax
Land Into the main Road Leading over at Vestal Gap and wee do
allow and Report as followeth Viz through Ezeckle Potts Land
thence through David Williams Land and John Rusel Land thence
Near the Line of Said Williams and Said Rusels line thence
through a Corner of John marvels Land thence through Even Evens
Land thence through Valintine millers and on or near the Line
Betwixt Said miller and John ferrels Land thence through
Henry mitchil Land Into the main Road Leading to Said Gap aginst
the Road that Leads Betwixt the mills to Robt hadgers ferry
also from the Said mill acors the Said Ezekiel Potts Land on
or near the Line Betwixt the Sd and Davd williams Land
to the mill Pen thence through Said Ezikiel Potts Land thence
through Nathans Potts Land thence through Thomas Quoslys
Land thence through thomas Shuelier Land to John osborn fence
Thence Twinity goals above the Said Land thence Down Said
osborn fence to the End of Said Land which wee return as a Riblick
Road to your Worships: as witness ours hand
September 7th 1771

Robt Jamison

Benjamin Hoff

In obedience to a Order of November Term 1770.
for a Road from Richard Thachers to Thomas Sheepards Mill
and we do allow and Report that the old Road shall be
continued and straightened from the end of said Thachers
Lane to said Mill, also from said Mill across said
Shepard Land and Wm Tates Land also through John Gragg
Land thence on the line betwixt s^d Gragg and John Brown
thence through Harmon Coxs land thence through a corner of
Land in possession of John Grant thence on the line
betwixt Timothy Howel and s^d Grant into the Main Road to
Leesburgh which we Return as a Publick Road to your
Worships as witness our Hands.

August 24, 1771   Thos X Pursley (his Mark)
                  Robt Jamison
                  Joshua Gore

(over)

Report of Road from & to Shepards
Mill. 1771

Septr 10th Ordered to be Established &
Thos Shepard app^d Surveyor thereof Leven
Powell to allot the hands & return the List

Road

Return of a Road from
and to Sheepards Mill
for Septem. Term
            1771

Road Case File # 43 1771
Loudoun County Circuit Court
Leesburg, Virginia

To the Selectmen to a Road of Rochester June 11th 1771

For a Road from Richard Hathwoods to Mathew Richards mill and also
to allow one Nesheet that the Road Made Recorded and Stated
from the End of said Hathwoods Land on the also from said mill bridge
said Rechards and Mr Hathwoods a turning to John Hoags Land
thence the line Betwixt D Hoag and goodn Browns thence through
Harmons Godard thence through a Corner of Land of Gershom Afhisons left
hand thence one the same Betwixt Timothy Howland and Richard Ross
Into the ways Road to Leebum at the Nethermost Ricketts Road
to your Worships as Witness our Hand

August D 28th 1771

[signatures]

To the worshipful Court of Loudoun County
James Mercer humbly showeth that the Road from
the Ford of Little River to Snickers's Gap & the
Road from the said Little River to Powells Mill
are both very prejudicial to your Petitioners
Plantation as they now go, & your Petitioner thinks
the inconveniencies may be removed by turning said
Roads & the public not injured, he therefore prays
that proper persons may be appointed to view &
report according to Law & c.

(over)

Mercers Petn

1771....to turn Roads
Septr 20th Order for View by
Fras Peyton Gt Cornels Bordine
Jacob Reid & Lewis Pearce or any three
upon Oath & report & c.

Road Case File # 43   1771
Loudoun County Circuit Court
Leesburg, Virginia

Dominion of Virginia Court of Loudoun County

James Moore humbly sheweth that whereas from the board of little runs for the road leading from Randall's Ford to Powell's ... from my dwelling to your petitioner's plantation with a narrow gap of your petitioners which may be used by turning said road by the public not thinking further pray that proper persons may be appointed to view & report accordingly to law &c

Miscellaneous Road Cases File No. 44, 1772
Clerk of Circuit Court
Archives
Leesburg, Virginia

To his Majesties Justices holding Court for the County of Loudoun County the 25th Day of may 1772

The Petition of John Vestal Samuel Potts and other inhabitants for a Road from Potts Mill across the Honorable George Wm Fairfax Esq Land into the Main Road leading over the Blue Ridge at Vestal Gap and your Worhips did Grant Review on the same and your Petitioners were assessed in tow of said Review and our opponents hath lately had a Review and a Road laid out which no way answers our first Petition as will offer by the Draft of the Place and your Petitioners Prays that another set of men might be appointed to View the difficult courses in the ground which will very plain offer that we your Petitioners doth not complain without a cause and your Petitioners as in duty bound shall ever Pray.

Simon Mathew	Casper Quik	John Vestal
Ezekiel Potts	John Fairey(?)	Samuel Potts
Nathan Potts	Larrance Swanck	Robt Jamison
John Osburn Senior	Conard Shanks	
John Osburn Junior	John Clice	
Artha McChristey	David Potts	
David Newhouse	Charles Hole	
Thos Jones	Richard Osburn	
J____ief Misal(?)		
Francis Scooling		

(over)

The Petition for a Road
Vestal & others
       O. Viewer   I. Thomson

Pet. of sundry for a Road
May 29 1772
Ordered that the way be Reviewed by James Hamilton, Israel Thompson, John Cavens & Saml Hill or any three upon Oath and Report & ___

(continued)

Road Case File # 44 1772
Loudoun County Circuit Court
Leesburg, Virginia

To his Majesties Justices of His said Court for the County of Loudon
County the 25th Day of May 1772.

The Petition of John Vestal Samuel Potts and other Inhabitants
of Shelburn Parish ——— Humbly Sheweth ———

That your Petitioners this May Court was a year Petitioned for
a Road from Potts mill across the Honorable George Wm Fairfax
Land into the main Road leading over the Blue Ridge at Vestal's
Gaps and your Worships did Grant Revuers on the Same and your
Petitioners was appointed for two of said Revuers and our oppotents
Goth Lofty had a Revuer and the Road laid out which as way answers
our first Petition as well as the other by the [illegible] of the Place
[illegible line]
Very plain to offer that we in the [illegible] District Complain
without a Cause and your Petitioners as in Duty Bound Shall
Ever Pray

John Vestal
Simon [illegible]   Samuel Potts
Ezekiel Potts   Robt Jannison
Nathan Potts
John Osburn Senr   John Slice
John Osburn Junior [illegible] Potts
Aitha McCurdry   [illegible] Hole
[illegible]   Richard Osburn

[Diagram:]
the Blue Ridge
the Way that your Petitioners wants the Road
the main Road
Johns own main road
The Short Hill

(continued)

The Draft

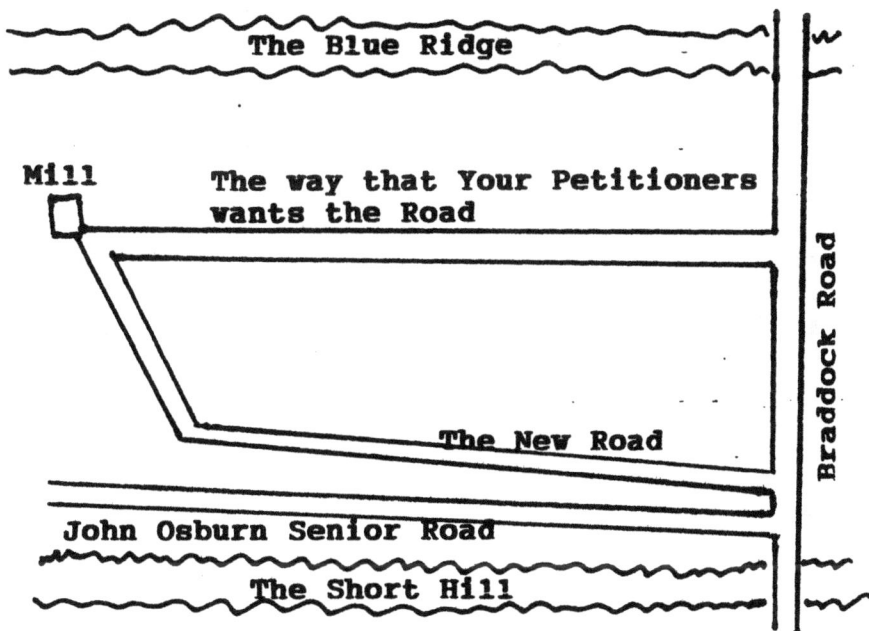

An attachment to the Petition for a Road from Vestal & Others dated May 25th, 1772 : A reproduction by Roberto Costantino, 2002

Road Case File # 44   1772
Loudoun County Circuit Court
Leesburg, Virginia

Upon a Petition of sundry inhabitants praying for a
Road from Israel Thompsons Mill the most convenient
and direct way through the Neighborhood and from
thence keeping nearly the same course passing through
or near Benjamin Pools Plantation till it intersects
the Road leading from Leesburg to Williams's Gap.
It is Ordered that Jonathan Myers William Wildman
Andrew Orason and John Schooley or any three of them
being first duly sworn and affirmed as the case may
be View the way Petitioned for and report to the
Court the conveniency and inconveniencies that may
attend the same.

       Test Cha's Binns ClCur

(over)

18 Augt 1772
Then the within named
persons were Qualified before
  Ja^s Hamilton

Road to be Viewed from
Thompsons Mill & c.

Road Case File # 44 1772
Loudoun County Circuit Court
Leesburg, Virginia

Loudoun County Court April the 28th 1772

Upon a Petition of sundry Inhabitants praying a View for a Road from Capel Thompsons Mill the most convenient and near way through the Neighbourhood and from Henry Keppings nearly the same course passing through Benjamin Bolzglandin Ishmaelacars the Road nearly the same course to William Greggs and thence to Jonathan Myers Abraham Wilhoan Andrew Oaxens the Shooley or any three of them being first Sworn in appears in the case may View the any Petitions for and report to the Court the conveniency and inconveniencies that may attend the same.

Test Chas Binns Cler

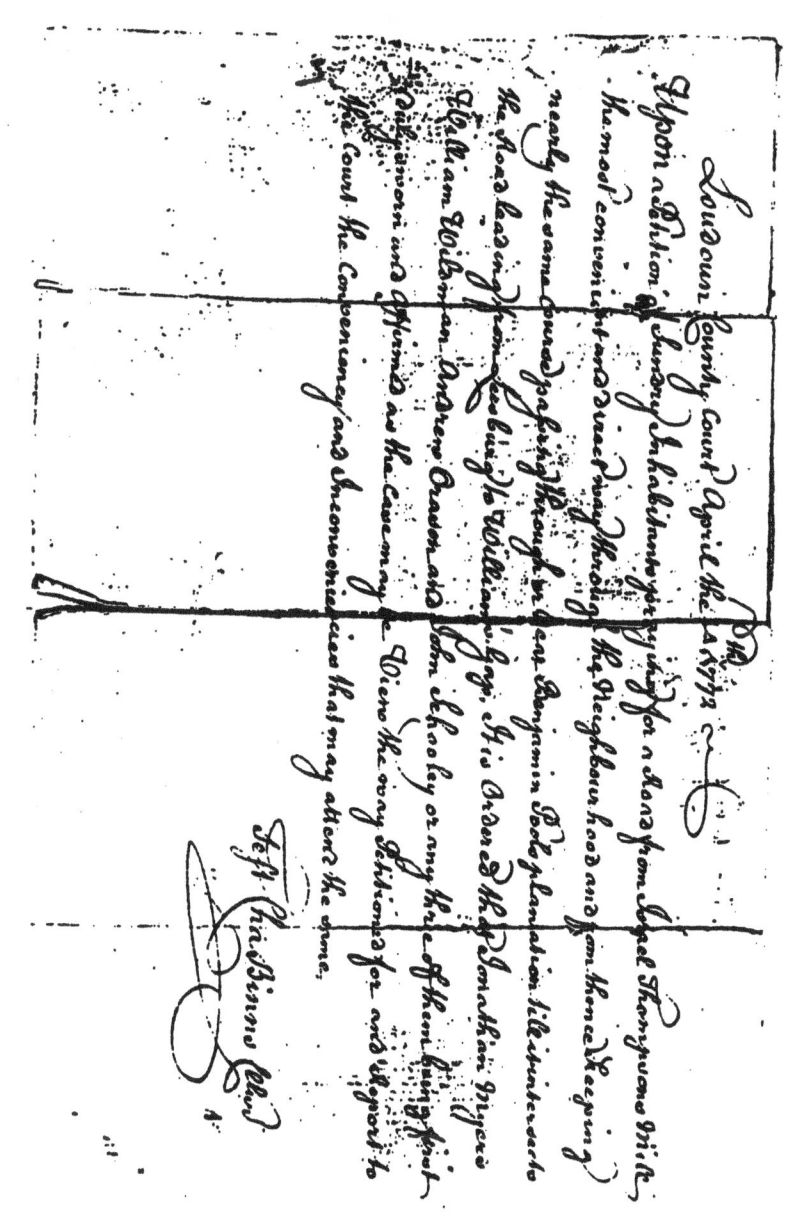

Loudoun County Court   April the 13th 1772

Upon a Petition of Thomas West setting forth that the
Great Road leading from Ashbys Gap to Belhaven by
running through his place renders it very detrimental
to him, and that the same may be turned a better way
& the distance much the same. It is Ordered that
William Rust, William Stephens, Joseph Gibson and
Isaac Gibson or any three of them being first duly
sworn before a Justice of the Peace View the way
Petitioned for and Report to the Court the
conveniencies and inconveniencies that may attend the
same.
                    Test.   Cha's Binns ClCur

Loudoun Sct
    Joseph Gibson   Isaac Gibson
    Sworn before me to View the above mentioned Road
    Given under my hand this 20th Day of August 1772
                            Wm Smith

(over)

Wm Stephens Sworn before
Mr Thos Lewis and Certified
to me
          Wm Smith

Road to be Viewed
for Thomas West

Road Case File # 44   1772
Loudoun County Circuit Court
Leesburg, Virginia

Loudoun County Court April the 10th 1770

Upon the Petition of Thomas Woorsetting forth that Loudoun from Ashbys Gap to Balls Road by running through his plantation at Loudon and that as the same may be turned a better way the out side of the same, It is Ordered that William Russ, William Stephens, Joseph Gibson and Jase Gibson or any three of them being first duly sworn before a Justice of the peace, view the Rhoad for any alterations that may be made for the convenience that may be there and Report to the Court the same.

Test
And Binns Clk

Loudoun Sct.

This is to Certify Gibson Isaac Gibson & —— were
sworn before me to View the above mentioned Road
Given under my hand this 20th Day of August 1770
West Sorrell

22 Day of August 1772

We the appointed Viewers of the new Road by Thos Wests have Viewed it and think it to be as good or better than the old Road.

      Wm Stephens
      Joseph Gibson
      Isaac Gibson

(over)

Wests Road Report
_____

1772 Augt 24 Established according to Report

Road Case File # 44   1772
Loudoun County Circuit Court
Leesburg, Virginia

To the worshipful Court of Loudoun County

The Petition of sundry inhabitants thereof humbly showeth, that Samuel Canby erected a convenient Grist Mill, the inhabitants living between the Beaver Dam Branch of Goose Creek, and the Northwest Fork thereof. But for want of a Road laid out and Established by your Worships, the said inhabitants are put to much inconvenience in getting to and from said Mill. If your Worships could think proper to apoint a suitable number of men, to view and lay out a Road from said Mill by Thomas Griggs Potter to the Great Road, leading from Sniggars Gap (Snickers Gap) to Alexandria by James Martins. Your Petitioners as in duty bound shall ever pray.

James Megeach
Joseph Parker
Anthony Bewley
John Coleman
Isaac Walker
Benjn Barton
Jonathan Ewer
William Boorom
Joseph Milner
Andrew Coombs
James Morrison
Thomas Mathews
William Rice
Gilbirt Vansikkel
Emanewel Cellum

(over)

Petition for a Road to Canbys Mill
Aug. 24th, 1772 Ordered that Thos Gregg potter, Isaac Sanders & Spencer Cooper do View on Oath and Report & co.

Petition for a Road
Commenced for the neighbors to Saml. Canby's Mill

   Thos Gregg potter
   Isaac Sanders
   Spencer Cooper

Road Case File # 44   1772
Loudoun County Circuit Court
Leesburg, Virginia

To the worshipful Court of Loudon County

The petition of sundry Inhabitants thereof humbly Sheweth, that Samuel Canby hath erected a convenient grist Mill, to the Inhabitants living between the Beaver dam Branch of goose Creek, and the northwest fork thereof, But for want of a Road laid out and Established by your worships, the said Inhabitants are put to much inconvenience in geting to and from said mill. If your worships could think propper to appoint a suitable number of men, to veiw and lay out a Road from said mill by Thomas Griggs, father to the great Road, leading from Sniggers gap to Alexandria by James Martins, your petitioners as in duty bound shall ever pray.

James Megeath
Joseph Parker
Anthony Bewley
John Colemail
Isaac Walker
Benj.ⁿ Barton
Jonathan Ewer
William Brown
Joseph Milner
James Mason
Andrew Coombs
James Morrison
Thomas Mathews
William Rice
Gillie Hensikka
Emanuel Cellum

Pursuant to an Order of Court to us directed We the Subscribers have Viewed the way therein mentioned and find there may be a good Road had with small expense Beginning at or turning out of Payns Road at a small Locust Tree in the edge of Jacob Shoemakers Field and from their the directest way through the Barley to his Barn then with his Lane the way now in use to the Corner of Jacob Hibbs Field then with the Line between said Hibbs & Daniel Lovatt to the Corner of Geo. Shaffers Lot then on the Line between said Shaffer and Geo. Nixons to the Corner of the said Nixons Wheat Field and from their the most direct way to Israel Thompsons Mill.____ As Witness our Hands this twenty seventh Day of May_____ 1772.

       John McIlhaney
        his
      Thomas X Pursell
        mark
      Samuel Gregg

(over)

Report of a Road
Viewed by
Jno McIlhanney
Saml Gregg
Thos Pursell

Ret^d & Order (illegible) out May Court 1772 (vida minutes)

Is. Thompson

1772 Augt 25 Established per Report Jacob Shoemaker app^d Surveyor John McIlhaney to allot the hands

---

Road Case File # 44 1772
Loudoun County Circuit Court
Leesburg, Virginia

Pursuant to an order of court to us directed We the Subscribers have viewed the way therein mentioned and find the way to a Good Road and with small expence Beginning at or Running out of Ryans Road at or near the edge of Arundels field and from thence the nighest way through the Barkery to his Barn then with his land the man in his field then the property land from thence with the Side between Toler & Daniels Road to the Crossing between Toler & Daniels Road from thence between Toler and Shafer and from thence between Shafer Pithams & Lee & between Lee & Shafer and his sons & to Sermons the said Ream Wharton Bradford Ricketts Direct way to Ewards Kingham's Mill we certified & signed this twenty Seventh Day of July —— 1779

John Wesley
Thomas X Fensel
  his mark
Samuel Gray

Pursuant to an order of Court to us directed We the Subscribers have Viewed the way for a Road from Israel Thompsons Mill to the Road leading from Leesburgh to Snickers Gap, and find there may be a good Road had, Beginning at said Thompson's Mill and from the end of his Lane a direct way with or near the Line between Isaac Thompson and George Tingle, and passing through the Lot late of Thomas Townsend keeping nearly the same course to a Lot now in possession of Craven Peyton and their crossing the Kittocton Creek at an old Ford, at the lower end of his Meadow, and then going between the Lands of John Davis and John Bishop only crossing a Corner of said Bishop's Land, by a Spring Head, on the right hand, then nearly with the Lines of Elisha Marks & Amos Goodwin then through a Corner of Mercer Brown's Land, to Isaac Nichols Junior on the left hand, and from their passing between the Land of Mahlon Kirkbride and William Nichols, then between the Lands of Samuel Iden and John Pickett passing near the House where Joseph Hart now liveth, and from thence to the lower Corner of Benjamin Po___ Meadow, and from their a direct way into the Road from Leesburgh to Snicker's near to Nathan Spencers Goose Pond, and do not find that it will be attended with any considerable inconveniency to any but are of opinion it may be very useful to a number of inhabitants.

    Robert Jamison   Wm Wildman
    Thomas Pursley   Jonathan Myers
    Joshua Gore   Andrew Orison
    Samuel Potts   John Skooley

(over)

Report of a Road from
Thompson's Mill & c.

Aug. 26th, 1772 Ordered to be reviewed by Robt Jamieson, Josh^a Gore, Saml Potts, Thos Pursley or any three & report on Oath & c.

Road Case File # 44 1772
Loudoun County Circuit Court
Leesburg, Virginia

PURSUANT to an order of Court to us directed We the Subscribers have Vaiwed the way for a Road from Israel Thompson Mill to the Road Leading from Leesburgh to Snikers Gap, and find there may be a Good Road had, BEGINNING at Said Thompson's Mill and from the End of his Lane a direct way with or near the line between Isaac Thompson and George Tingle, and passing through the Lott late of Thomas Townsend keeping nearly the same Course to a Lott now in Possession of Craven Peyton and there crossing the Kittocton Creek at an old Ford, at the Lower End of his Meadow, and then Going into or on the lands of John Davis and John Bishop only crossing a corner of Said Bishops Land, by a Spring Head, on the Right Hand, then Nearly with the lines of Elisha Marks & Amos Goodwin then through a corner of Moses Browns Land, to Isaac Nichols Junior on the left Hand, and from there passing Between the Land of Mahlon Kirkbride and William Nichols, Then Between the Lands of Samuel Iden and John Rickett passing Near the House where Joseph Hart now Liveth, and from thence to the Lower Corner of Benjamin Bur[?] Meadow, and from there a Direct way into the Road from Leesbur[gh] to Sniker's, near to Nathan Spencers Gorse Pond, and do not fin[d] that it will be attended with any Considerable Inconveniency [but] But are of Opinion it may be very Usefull to a number of Inhabita[nts]

Robert Jamison
Thomas Pursley
Joshua Gore
Samuel Potts

Wm. Wildman
Jonathan Myers
Andrew Orison
John S Wooley

To the Worshiful Court of Loudoun

    The Petition of the Subscribers humbly showeth, that about two years ago your Worships Granted an Order for the Opening a Road from the Blue Ridge at Oldacris Mill to Leven Powells Mill which was desired for the benefit of your Petitioners general but for some material reasons it would be much to the advantage of ye Petitioners to have the said Road turned, to have the Road as it now stands at Thos Drakes Meadow & to go in a direct course to Hezekiah Guys Grist Mill & near the Quaker Meetinghouse, thence to cross Goose Creek at James Smiths & to keep that old Road to the said Powells Mill and, the advantages arising from this change would be first making the distance much shorter, secondly, giving an easy passage to and from the said Mill & Meetinghouse which is much wanting, the ways at present being very difficult, Your Worships taking the premises under consideration & Granting such relief as you shall think just. Your Petitioner will as in duty bound ever pray &___

Joseph Cumins	Thomas Smith
John Dunlap	Hezekiah Guy
Charles West	Samuel Guy
James Hail	William Olakers
James Carter	John Olakers
Jacob Freizell	Samuel Niles
Malakiah Comings	William Oldakers
John Lemons	Joseph Hoge
John Gibson	Thomas Drake
Moses Gibson	William Neal
Thomas Gibson	Joseph Fred
William Rust	

(over)

Thomas Smith
Thomas Russell
James leith
Isaac Cogill

Pet for Road   1772
Sept. 28th Read and Ordered
a View by Thomas Smith
Tho. Russell James Leith &
Isaac Cogill or any three of them
& Report & ___

Road Case File # 44   1772
Loudoun County Circuit Court
Leesburg, Virginia

To The Worshipful Court of the County of Loudoun, ffc

The Petition of sundry the Subscribers Humbly Sheweth, That about two years ago your Worships granted an order for the opening a road from the Blue Ridge at Ole[a]cris's Mill to Leven Powells Mill, which was designed for the benefit of your Petitioners in General, but for some material reasons it would be much to the advantage of sd Petitioners to have the said Road Turned to leave the road as it now stands at Thos Drakes Meadow & to go a direct course to Hezekiah Guys Grist Mill & near the Quaker Meeting house, thence to Cross Goose Creek at James Leiths & to keep the old road to the said Powells Mill road. The advantages arriving from this Change would be first making the distance much shorter, Secondly, giving an easy passage to and from ~~~ Guys Meeting house which is much wanting, the ways at present being very difficult. Your Worships taking the Premises under consideration & granting such relief as you shall think Just, & your Petitioners will as in duty bound ever pray &c.

Joseph Cumins   Thomas Smith
John Dunkin   Ezekiah Guy
Charles West   Samuel Guy
James [illegible]   William Baker
James Carter   John Baker
Jacob Reed   Samuel Niles
Malakiah Cumins   William Bristow
John Cumins   Henry [illegible]
John Gibson   Joseph [illegible]
Moses Gibson   Thomas Drake
Thomas Gibson   William Neal
William Rust   Joseph Neal
James Leith

To the Worshiful Court of Loudoun

This is to inform your Worships that your Petitioner desires your Worships to grant him an Order to turn the Roads that leads by his Fence for about the distance of three hundred yards the Road now running much to the damage of this your Petitioner and it will be as near and as good a way as where it now runs & this is what your Petitioner prayeth and shall pray & c.

N.B. It is the Church Road that leads from Evens's Shop at Shugerland Run to Broad Run Church.

November the 23, 1772   William Horsman

(over)

Ordered that John Piles, Joshua Evins, Richard Spurr and James Whaley or any three View the within ment^d Road and Report & c.

O. to View Road

Horsmans Petition
_____

1772 Novr O. John Piles, Jos^a Evans Richd Spurr & James Whaley or any three on Oath View & Report & c.
_____

Road Case File # 44 1772
Loudoun County Circuit Court
Leesburg, Virginia

To the Worshipful Court of Chatham Training

This is to inform your Worships that your petitioner Desires Worships to grant him an order to turn the Road that Leads by his fence for about the Distance of three hundred yards the Road now Running much to the damage of this your petitioner and it will be as near and as good a way as where it now runs and it is what your petitioner prays &c.

N.B. As it is the Church Road that Leads from Cicero's Bridge to the ford in Haw River to Spring-Friends Church

November the 29 1772

William Horsman

In pursuance of an Order of Court to us directed
we being first Sworn to View the Way Petitioned
for by sundry inhabitants from the Valindine
Quarter to Farling Balls Mill do find that it
will be convenient to go with or near the old
Road as far as Lanord Mays Fence from their a
direct course by Moses Heatons to s^d Mill &
Store.

              John Heatton
    Given under our hands
    this 26th Day Novr 1772 Joseph Bohen

Moses Heatton   Moses Heatton
or Saml Schooley
Samuel

(over)

Report of a Road from
the Valentine Quarter & c.

1772 Novr 27, ret^d Established
Moses Heaton Surveyor &
J^o Hamilton to allot hands

Report of a Road

Road Case File # 44 1772
Loudoun County Circuit Court
Leesburg, Virginia

the performance of our note & Covenant to aid Benj'd to the
Bears and if William to our the Day for the land they
fulfill out herein the valuation price. For the Land,
and if not—of and that it shall be convenient to spend in Bass
near the old Rad as has a Land may hence fore with
their a Dynect conveying where shall out to said
& that

Signed Sealed & (Samuel Hatton
Delivered (
in our Presence (Nahum Hatton
Lorenzo

In under our hand
this 26th day Oct 1799   S. Peabody

Miscellaneous Road Cases File No. 45, 1773
Clerk of Circuit Court
Archives
Leesburg, Virginia

These are to acquaint the Honorable Gentlemen of
Loudoun Court that I your humble Petitioner am much
dissatisfied and like to be greatly damaged by a late
laid out Road coming through my Land in a form I
shall show you below Your Petitioner begs the favor of
Your Honors to take this matter in consideration and
prevent this damage I am also of opinion the Road
might be laid off on better ground and more convenient
to ye neighborhood for which favor your Petitioner
shall ever be in duty bound to pray.

Thomas Pursley   Henory Mikil

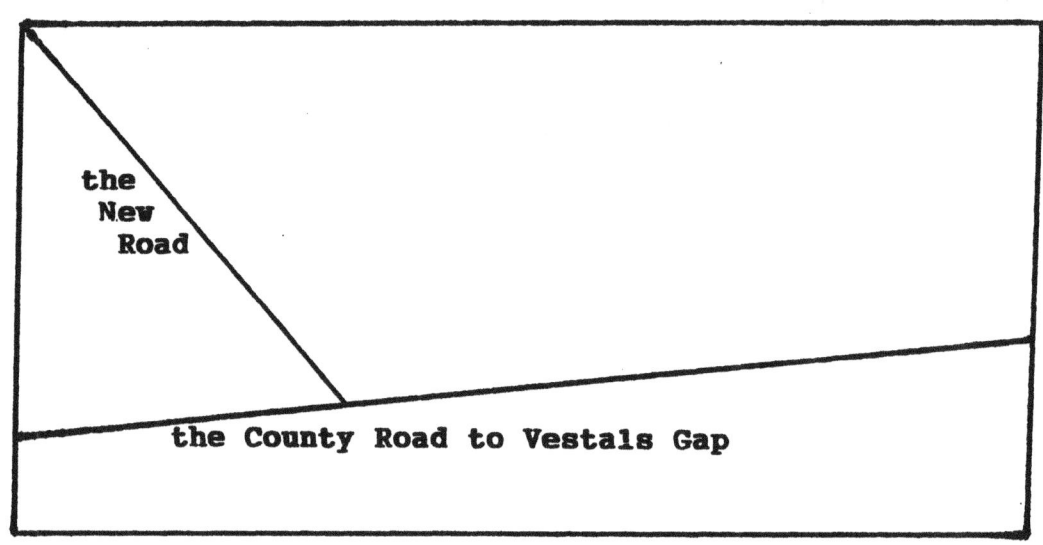

(over)

Petition for Road by
    Henry Michael

Road Case File # 45 1773
Loudoun County Circuit Court
Leesburg, Virginia

These are to acquaint the Honorable Gentlemen of ye
Loudoun Cort that I your Humble Partioner am much
Dissadisfyed and Like to be Greatly Damiged by a Late
Lay out Road Comming through my Land in a form I
Shall shew you below your Partioner Begs the feavour of
your honours to take this Matter in Consideration and
Prevent this Damage I am also of apinion the Road
Mout be Layd off on better Ground and more Conveniant
To ye nighberhood for which feavour your Partisioner
Shall Ever be in Duty Bound to Pray

Thomas Pursley   Hendry Mikil

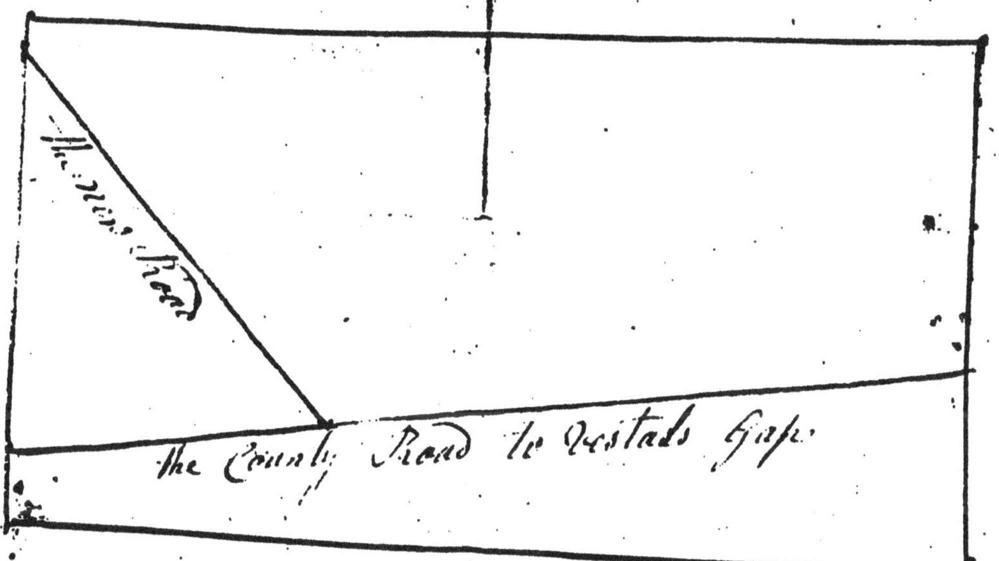
the new Road
the County Road to Vestals Gap

To the worshipful Court of Loudoun

The Petition of Henry Brown humbly prayeth that he may have a Road established from a Plantation of his near George Mann & Mecer Brown's by his present dwelling Home to Richd Roch Mill & shall Pray

        Henry Brown
        March 1773

(over)

H. Brown
Petition

for a Road
March 23, 1773 R. Williams
Far. Ball Jinkin Williams
& Isaac Sands to View & Report

        R. Williams
        Farlin Ball
        Jinkin Williams
        Isaac Sands

Brown's Petition for a Road

Road case File # 45 1773
Loudoun County Circuit Court
Leesburg, Virginia

To William Phillips Esqr of London

I, Robert Henry Brown Hamble Sprekitt that the
may have a Chapters from a Plantation will
then fergehams kennersbown by his Present
Dwelling House to their Roath Mile
A Mile from &c

Henry Brown
March 1773

In obedience to an Order of Loudoun County Court we
the Subscribers have Viewed the ground for a Road
from Josias Clapham's Plantation towards Leesburgh.
We are of oppinion the nearest & best way for it
is to go from the Corner of a young Orchard Fence
of his on a direct line to a Corner or Elbow of an
old Road near Samuel Irwin's ~~thence the nearest way
would be through the heart of a Tract of Land of
John Tramels into an old Road by a Branch near Thos.
George's Land thence along the said old Road into
Noland's Ferry Road by Jason Thomas's but circumstances
considered~~ we are of opinion it would suit all parties
better to continue the Road from the aforementioned
place near Saml Irwins on a straight line by a blazed
mark of trees to an old Road or Path near a Gate on the
Plantation where the sd Clapham now lives thence along
the sd old Road into Noland's Ferry Road at Jason
Thomas's & c.

                                               Jas Sanders
                                               William Woolard
Viewers Sworn   John St Clair
     Francis Peyton

(over)

Claphams
Report of a Road
Granted per Report
March 23d 1773

Josias Clapham has
Liberty to open the same

Road Case File # 45   1773
Loudoun County Circuit Court
Leesburg, Virginia

In Obedience to an Order of Loudoun Court we
the Subscribers have Viewd the Ground for a Road
from Josias Claphams Plantation toward Leesburg
We are of Opinion the nearest & best way for it
is to go from the corner of a young Orchard fence
of his on a direct Line to a corner or Elbow of an old road
near Samuel Irvins. ~~thence the nearest way would~~
~~be through the Meadow in Sam'l Island 10 to Iveull~~
~~into an old road by a branch near Sam'l Georges line~~
~~thence along the said old road into Potown ~~ ~~~~
~~~~ ~~but, on enquiry, we find~~
we are of Opinion it would suit all parties better to continue
the Road from the aforementioned place near Sam'd Irvins
on a straight Line by a Blazed Mark on Trees to an
old road, or path near a gate on the Plantation when the
s'd Irvin now lives thence along the s'd old Road
[illegible] _____

Viewers sworn   Ja'l Sanders
  Francis Peyton   William Woollard
                                            John S'l Piers

To the Worshipful Court of Loudoun County the Petition
of Benjamin Chandler humbly showeth,

That some time ago your Worships granted an Order to
View a way for a Road from Fauq. Line to Levin Powells
Mill Road, that on Viewing the said Road it was proposed
to him that if he would suffer the said Road to go
through his Plantation that the persons for whose benefit
the said Road was opened would be at the expense of
setting up & keeping in repair Gates where the Road should
go through his said Plantation, to which he consented tho'
much to his prejudice notwithstanding such engagement they
have hitherto failed to make the said Gates nor do they
intend to give themselves any trouble about them, Your
Petitioner therefore being a very poor Man & not able to
be at the expense of Gates himself, humbly prays that your
Worships would grant an order to View a way for the said
Road round your Petitioners Plantation, & ye Petitioner as
in duty bound shall ever pray & c.

Persons, Convenient for Viewers,
Wm Berkley, James Lampkin, & Benj. Rust.

(over)

Benj^a Chandlers
Petition for
to turn a Road

1773 March 23 Wm Berkly
James Lamkin & Benj^a Rust
to View and Report

Road Case File # 45
Loudoun County Circuit Court
Leesburg, Virginia

To The Worshipful Court of Loudoun County, the Petition of Benjamin Chandler Humbly Sheweth,

That some time ago your Worships granted an order to View a way for a road from Fauqr. Line to Levin Powells Mill road, that on Viewing the said road it was proposd to him that if he would suffer the said road to go through his plantation that the persons for whose Benefit the said road was opened would be at the expence of setting up & keeping in repair Gates where the road should go through his said plantation, to which he consented tho' much to his prejudice notwithstanding such engagement they have hitherto fail'd to make the said Gates nor do they intend to give themselves any trouble about them. Your Petitioner therefore, being a very poor man & not able to be at the expence of Gates himself Humbly prays that your Worships would grant order to View a way for the said Road round your Petitioners plantation, & yr Petitioner as in duty bound shall ever pray &c.

Persons Convenient for Viewers,
Wm Berkhly, James Lamphier, & Benjn Rust

This is to Certify that Mercer
Brown & George Tavener hath
been Qualified to View a Road wth
William Brown by an Order of
Loudoun County Court.

    Ja^s Hamilton
    6th April, 1773

Road Case File # 45   1773
Loudoun County Circuit Court
Leesburg, Virginia

This is to certify that Messrs Brown & George Lawrence hath laid Lindley's Old Pine creek Road off to William Brown by an order of Lycoming County Court

J. Hamilton
6th April 1773

Loudoun County Court   November the 24th 1772

    Upon the Petition of William Horsman for leave to turn a Road, Ordered that John Piles, Joshua Evans, Richard Spurr and James Whaley or any three of them being first duly sworn before some Justice of the Peace for this County do View the way Petitioned for, and Report to the Court the conveniencies or inconveniencies which may attend the same being turned.
                  Test   Cha's Binns ClCur

In obedience to an Order of Loudoun County Court hereunto annexed we the Subscribers being first Sworn have been and Viewed the Road Petitioned for by Wm Horseman that leads from Broad Run Church to Joshua Evans's Shop opposite to Wm Horseman's ____ find that the distance is near about the same, and that the Road may be made equally as good all but one small Hollow place which may be made good.

                              Richd Spurr
                              Joshua Evans
                              James Whealey

(over)

Loudoun Sct Feb. 19th 1773
Joshua Evans, Richd Spurr &
James Whaley was Sworn agreeable
to the within Order before me.
                Jno Coleman (Horseman)

April 26, 1773 Ret. & Established

Road to be Viewed
for Wm Horseman

Road Case File # 45   1773
Loudoun County Circuit Court
Leesburg, Virginia

Loudoun County Court November the 2d 1772.

Upon a Petition of William Horseman for leave to turn a Road, Ordered that John Piles, Joshua Evans, Richard Spurr and James Whaley or any three of them being first duly sworn before some Justice of the Peace for this County do View the Way Petitioned for, and Report to the Court the conveniencies or inconveniencies that may attend the same being turned.

Test Cha Binns Cl

In Obedience to an Order of Loudoun County Court hereunto Annext we the Subscribers being first Sworn have been and Viewed the Rode petitioned for by Wm Horseman that Leads from broadrun Church to Joshua Evans's Shop opposite to Wm Horseman's & Find that the Distance is Neare about the same, and that the Rode may be made Equaly as Good all but one small Hollow place which may be made Good

Richd Spurr
Joshua Evans
James Wheatey

Loudoun County Court   August the 25th 1772

It is Ordered upon a View returned by Thomas Cockrell and others that John Orr have leave to open a Road agreeable to the limits described in the Report, and that Anthony Russell, Fielding Turner and Benjamin Mason Report to the Court the sufficiency and insufficiency of the said Road when the same shall be completed by the said John Orr.

                Test. Cha's Binns Cl Cur

(over)

By virtue of the within Order to us directed we have Viewed the way and are of opinion the said John Orr may have liberty to turn the Road therein mentioned as being the most convenient way   Witness our hands 26 April 1773

                Anthony Russell
                Fielding Turner
                Benj Mason

    For
Mr John Orr

1773 April 26 Returned Estabd
Surveyor former Road to keep the
same in repair

Road Case File #45   1773
Loudoun County Circuit Court
Leesburg, Virginia

Loudoun County Court August the 13th 1759

It is Ordered upon a View taken by Francis Peyton Cockrell and others that John Orr have leave to open a Road agreeable to the Limits laid down in the Report, and that Anthony Russell, Jacob Treber, James Turner and Benjamin Mason Report to the Court the Sufficiency and insufficiency of the said Road when the same shall be compleated by the said John Orr

Test. Cha. Binns Clerk

To the Worshipfull Court of Loudoun County
The Petition of us the Subscribers humbly showeth
that whereas we the Subscribers being destitute of
a Road to go to Mill and Church and whereas there
may be made a Road without much labour or prejudice
to people from Capt Anthony Russel's or the Smith's
Shop thence with Capt Russel's Line to Broad Run to
Abraham Warford's Line and with s^d Line to Piney
Branch thence to Sampson Turley's Plantation thence
to Joseph and Daniel Reeder's Lines to the Mountain
Road at the Race Ground by John Boiles supposed to
be four miles and we the Subscribers think that a
Road thus laid out would be of great benefit to us
as well as to a number of others and hope your
Worships will take it into consideration and your
Petitioners shall ever Pray & c._____

Daniel Reeder	Anth^y Russell
Thomas Hubbell	Abram Warford
Joseph Reeder	Vincent Lewis
Thomas Lake	
David Reeder	
John Hoff	
Peter Acker	
(?) Craven	
Wm Beavers	

(over)

Petition for a Road
_____

1773 April 26 O. View by A. Russell
Abra. Warfurd & Vincent Lewis
_____

Road Case File # 45 1773
Loudoun County Circuit Court
Leesburg, Virginia

To the Worshipfull Court of Loudoun County

The Petition of us the Subscribers humbly Sheweth that whereas we the Subscribers being destitute of a Road to goe to mill and Church and whereas there may be maid a Road without much Labour or prejudice to People from Cap.t Anthony Russels to the mill Shop & thence with Cap.t Russels Line to Broad Run to Abraham Warfords Line and with s.d Line to Piney Branch thence to Sampson Turleys Plantation thence to Joseph and Daniel Reeders Lines to the mountain Road at the Race Ground by John Boiles Supposed to be four miles and we the Subscribers think that a Road thus laid out would be of great Benefit to us as well as to a number of others and hope your Worships will take it into Consideration and your Petitioners shall Ever Pray &c.

Daniel Reeder

Thomas Hutchell

Joseph Reeder

Thomas Lake

David Reeder

John Hoff

Peter Hiti

Phillip Brown

W.m Beavers

Anth.o Russell
Abram Warford
Vincent Lewis

145

To the Honourable Court of Loudoun County.
Whereas we the several Inhabitants of this Neighborhood
do think it would be very useful and convenient for us
to have a Road opened out of Abel Jenny's Road leading
to the Quaker Meetinghouse, to begin at or near Henry
Stone's and from thence leading by Archibald Murry's,
Alexander Ross and so to Farling Balls Mill, therefore
do humbly request that your Honours will appoint
Viewers and your Petitioners will as in duty bound
Pray & .

Daniel Matheny	Abel Janney
Joseph Hutton	John Phillips
Joseph Hibs	Samuel Gregg
Jerrol Holand	James Tobin
Andrew Thompson	Thomas Tobin
Robert Gregg	James French
Richard Gregg	Elijah Houghton
Junis Petters	
William Hill	
Wᵐ Matheny	
John Dorsitt	~~for Viewers Abel Janney~~
(?) (?)	~~Junis Petters~~
(?) (?)	~~Joseph Hutton~~
	~~Alexander Ross~~

Phil. Noland
Wᵐ Douglass } Gent.
John Sinkler
John Todhunter

(over)

Petition for a Road

1773 April 27ᵗʰ Order for View by
Phil Noland, William Douglass Gent.
John Sinkler & John Todhunter or
any three upon Oath

Road Case File # 45   1773
Loudoun County Circuit Court
Leesburg, Virginia

To the Honourable Court of Loudoun County —

Whereas we the several Inhabitants of this Neighbourhood do think it wou'd be very usefull and convenient for us to have a Road opened out of Abel Jenny's Road (leading to the Quaker Meetinghouse) to begin at or near Henry Stones and from thence leading by Archibald Murray's, Alexander Ross and so to Farling Balls Mill, Therefore do humbly request that your Honours will appoint Viewers and your Petitioners will as in duty bound Pray &c —

Daniel Matheny	Abel Janney
Joseph Hutton	John Phillips
Joseph Hill	Samuel Gregg
Jacob Noland	James Jobin
Andrew Thompson	Thomas Jobin
Richard Gregg	James French
John Gregg	Elijah Houghton
Tunis Betts	
William Hill	
Wm Matheny	
John Dorret	Abel Janney
	David Potters
	Joseph Hutton
	Alexander Ross
	Phil. Noland } Gent
	Wm Douglass
	John Sinkler
	John Todhunter

147

Loudoun County Court

March 23^{d}, 1773

Ordered that Nathan Spencer, George Tavener, William Brown & James Best or any three (who being first Qualified before some magistrate for this County) do View the most convenient way for a Road from Mahlon Janney's Mill to the Main Road by Nathan Spencer's and make Report thereof to the Court of conveniencies and inconveniencies that may attend the same.

      Test
        Cha's Binns Cl Cur

(over)

Loudoun Sc^{t}
  by virtue of the within Order we have Viewed the within Road & think a Road may be got without prejudice to any body agreeable (?) we have marked witness our hands.
      Nathan Spencer
      Geo. Tavenner
      William Brown

Loudoun Sc^{t}
  Nathan Spencer George Tavener & William Brown being three of those People called Quakers was Qualified to make a just report of the within Road this 10 May 1773 before
      William Douglass

May 10th, 1773 Returned and Established per Report

Spencer & c.
to View a Road

Road Case File # 45 1773
Loudoun County Circuit Court
Leesburg, Virginia

Loudoun County Court   March 23rd 1773

Ordered that Nathan Spencer, George Taylor, William Brown & James
Bait or any three (who being first Qualified before some Magestrate for this
County) do View the most Convenient way for a road from Mahlon Janney's
Mill to the Main road by Nathan Spencer's and make report thereof to the
Court of Conveniencies and inconveniencies that may attend the same
                                         Test Cha: Binns Clerk

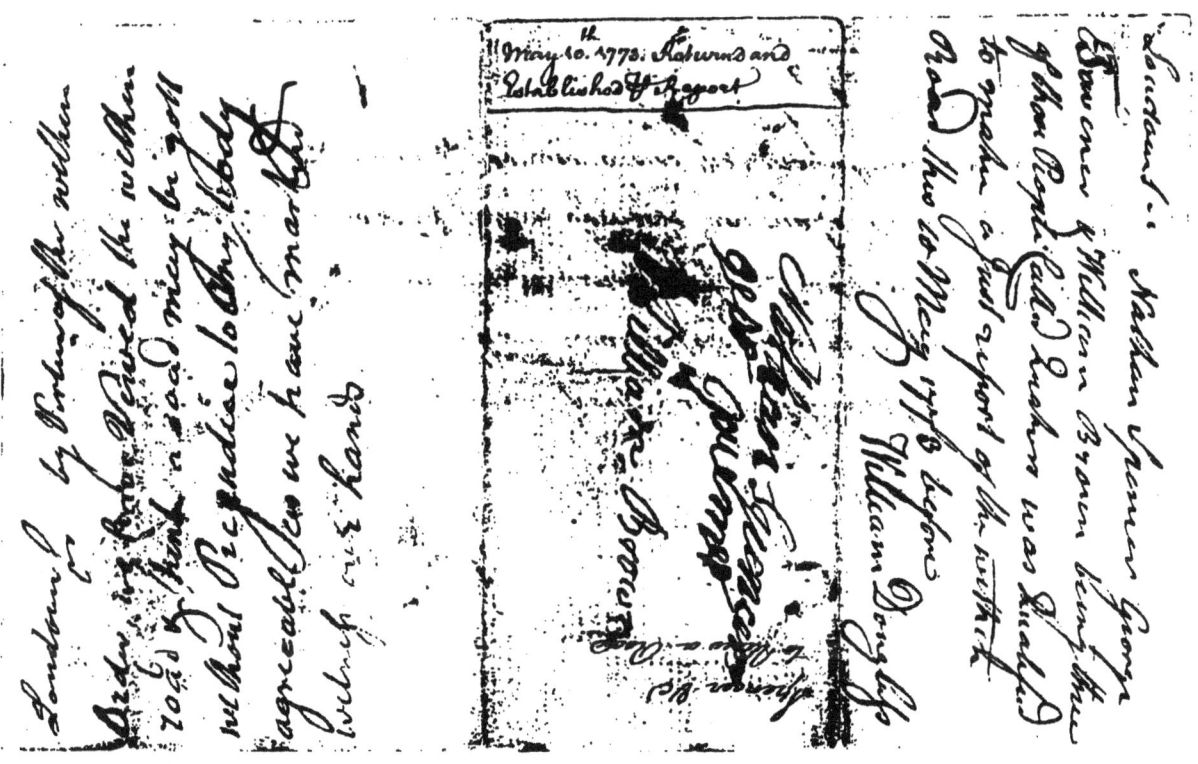

May 10th 1773. Returns and Established the Report

Loudoun ss: Nathan Spencer, George
Taylor & William Brown being three
of the People called Quakers was Qualified
to make a just report of the within
Road this 10 May 1773 before
                              William Douglass

Loudoun ss by Virtue of the within
Order we have viewed the within
Road & think a road may be got
without Prejudice to any body
agreeable as we have marked
Witness our hands

To the Worshipfull Court of Loudoun County

The Petition of the Vestry of Cameron Parish humbly showeth, that they are now building a Church near Sugarland Run in the Parish aforesaid. And prays that they may have the Road leading from Broad Run Church to Sugarland Run turn'd by the s'd new Church. And shall pray & c._____

Jeremiah Hutchison
John Moss } C.W.

Fran's Peyton
W'm Smith
Simon Hancock
Tho's Lewis } Viewers

(over)

Petition of the Vestry
of Cameron Parish
for a Road by the new
Church

Aug't 11   Order for View

1773

Road Case File # 45 1773
Loudoun County Circuit Court
Leesburg, Virginia

To the Worshipfull the Court of Loudoun County

The Petetion of the Vestry of Cameron Parish Humbly Sheweth. That they are now Building a Church Near Sugarland Run in the Parish aforesaid. And prays that they may have the Road leading from Broadrun Church to Sugarland Run turn'd by the s'd New Church. And shall pray &c.

Jeremiah Hutcheson

John Moss J.C.W.

Fran's Peyton
W'm Smith
Simon Hancock
Tho' Lewis
} Vestors

To the Worshipful Court of Loudoun County

    John Alexander humbly showeth. That your Pet^r is in want of a Road for a wagon to run from his house to Mr George Wests Lane, and prays your Worships to appoint such persons as you may think proper to View the way and report the conveniency and inconveniencies that may attend the same, to your Worshis, & your Pet^r shall pray & c.

Wm Cotton Senr
Wm Whitiley
George Taler
Francis Elgin

(over)

John Alexander Pet^o
for an outlet to Geo. Wests
Lane

1773 Augt 11th Ordered
that Wm Cotton Senr,
Wm Whitely, George Taylor
and Francis Elgin View the
way and report & c.

Road Case File # 45   1773
Loudoun County Circuit Court
Leesburg, Virginia

To the Worship the Court of Loudoun County

John Alexander Humbly Sheweth. That your Petitioner is in want of a Road
from Waggon to run from his House the George Town Lane and prays your
Worships to appoint such persons as you may think proper to view the
way and report the convenience and inconveniences that may attend the same
and your Petitioner as in duty bound shall pray &c

Wm Carrodine
Wm Whiteley
George Taber
Francis Elgin

We the Subscribers agreeable to the appointment of the Worshipful Court have viewed the grounds about Tuskarora and are of opinion that the Road may be turned to the public advantage, but will at first be attended with some considerable labour, which way we have made some small marks, but cannot so describe it to your Worships as to make you sufficiently sensible, tho' we are ready to show the Surveyor or persons appointed to open the same, the way we have pitched upon whenever thereunto required. Given under our hands this 4th day of september 1773.

Persons to show the way to the Surveyor of the Road

Craven Peyton
Josiah Maffitt
Nathan Baker

(over)

Report Road Tuscarora

1773 Septr 14th ret^d & Established & the Viewers to show the Surveyor the way marked by them.

Road Case File # 45 1773
Loudoun County Circuit Court
Leesburg, Virginia

We the Subscribers agreeable to the appointment of the Worshipfull Court have viewed the ground about Eskeene and are of opinion that the Road over it turned to the public advantage but will at first be attended with repairable labour, which my we have made with which we have done. We ??? to your Worship as to make you sufficiently sensible, this we are ready to shew the Surveyor or person appointed to goe the same, the day and hour fixed upon whenever thereunto required. Given under our hands this 6th day of September 1793.

(Servants & any thereof to the Surveyor of the Road)

Baxter Peyton
J Fish Moffett
Thomas Baker

Pursuant to an Order of the Worshipful Court of Loudoun County Dated the 11th Day of October 1773 to us directed, to view the most convenient way for a Road, to be cleared from the Mountain Road near the Church, to Mr Tripletts Mill and near Jacob Reads, We are of opinion that the said Road ought to begin at the Lane between Garrett and McGeach and keep near their Line the way shown by Isaac Sanders to the Great Bend of the South West Fork of Goose Creek, and from thence between the Plantation of Fitzsimmons and the Widow Williams, down a Ridge to the said Mill, and from the Mill up the side of the Mountain near Mr Tripletts House into the old Road, and continue the old Road to the Plantation of William McNabb and then through his Plantation near his House in to the old Road again, which must be continued to the Plantation of Jacob Read, and round his Fence the way cleared by him, into the Mountain Road, As Witness our Hands this 6th Day of November 1773.

                                          Wm Bronaugh
                                          Thomas Chinn
                                          Thomas Marbury

(over)

Road Viewed from
Mountain Road to Triplet's & c.

1773 Novr 6th Established
per Report. Francis Triplett
appointed Surveyor and
Francis Peyton to allot
the hands.

Road Case File # 45   1773
Loudoun County Circuit Court
Leesburg, Virginia

Pursuant to an Order of the Worshipful Court of Loudoun County, Dated the 11th Day of October 1773. to us directed, to review the most convenient way for a Road, to be cleared from the Mountain Road near the Church, to Mr. Triplett's Mill and near Jacob Read's, We are of opinion that the said Road ought to begin at the Lane between Garrett and McGeath and keep near their line the way shewn by Isaac Sanders to the great bent of the South West Fork of Goose Creek, and from thence between the Plantations of Fitzsimmons and the Widow Williams, down a ridge to the said Mill, And from the Mill up the side of the Mountain near Mr. Triplett's House into the old Road, and continue the old Road to the Plantation of William McNabb and then through his Plantation near his House in to the old Road again, which must be continued to the Plantation of Jacob Read, and round his Fence the way cleared by him, into the Mountain Road, As Witness our Hands this 6th Day of November 1773.

Wm. Bronaugh
Thomas Chinn
Thomas Marbury

Loudoun County Court, October the 11th 1773

Upon a motion of Simon Triplet Gent. It is again Ordered that William Bronaugh, Thomas Chinn and Thomas Marbury Review the most convenient way for a Road, to be cleared from the Mountain Road near the Church to the said Triplett's Mill and near Jacob Reid's and Report again to the Court the conveniency and inconveniencies that may attend the same.

                    Test
                        Cha's Binns Cl Cur

(over)

Road to be Viewed
for Simon Triplet Gent.

1773 Nov. 8th return

Loudoun County Court. October the 11, 1773.

Upon a motion of Simon Triplet Gent, It is again Ordered, That William Brounaugh, Thomas Chinn and Thomas Marbury Review the most convenient way for a Road, to be cleared from the Mountain Road near the Church to the said Triplett's Mill and near Jacob Reids and Report again to the Court the Conveniency and Inconveniencies that may attend the same

Test Cha: Binns Clk

Road to be Viewed
for Simon Triplet Jun.
1773 Now a return

In the Year 1770 I obtained an Order of this Court for a View of a Road from Morris's Ford of Goose Creek to the Main Road leading from Dawson's Ford of Goose Creek to Leesburg._____ The Viewers appointed by the Court were Nich^s Minor Stephen Donaldson & Fleming Patterson Gent^n ___ Those Gent^n I never could get together since, so most humbly pray your Worships to appoint other Viewers.

(over)

   Wm Dugliss
   Wm Mead
   Francis Elgin
   Isaac Fouch

   or any three

Road to be Viewed
from Dawson's to Leesburg
_____

1773 Novr 10 O^d for View
_____

Road Case File # 45 1773
Loudoun County Circuit Court
Leesburg, Virginia

At the Year 1770 Johnson amoverst the Court for a view of and from Morris's Ford of Deep Creek to the Main road leading from Dawson's Ford of Deep Creek to Hillsborough — The Viewers appointed by the Court were Nicholas Moor, Stephen @naudon, Fleming, Bellmon Gates — Thomas Gates Esqr. Ordered by this Court to be most Humbly pray now—Worship to appoint other Viewers

Miscellaneous Road Cases File No. 46, 1774
Clerk of Circuit Court
Archives
Leesburg, Virginia

Loudoun   Octo. Court 1773

Ordered that Thomas West, Thomas Owsley, James Lewis and William Robinson or any three who being first duly Qualified before some Magistrate for the said County do View the most convenient way for a Road to be cleared from or near Ashbys Gap to John Gibsons Mill and from thence into the Road leading to Alexandria, and that they Report to the Court the conveniencies and inconveniencies that may attend the same.

    Test
     Cha's Binns Cl. Court

(over)

Loudoun Sct
  Thos Owsley, James Lewis, & William Robinson
 Sworn this 10th of March 1774, Before

       Thos Lewis

    Road to be Viewed
    for Mr Gibson

Road Case File # 46 1774
Loudoun County Circuit Court
Leesburg, Virginia

Loudoun Octo. Court 1772

Ordered that Thomas West, Thomas Cureley, James Lewis and William Robinson or any three who being first duly Qualified before some Magistrate for the said County do View the most Convenient way for a Road to be cleared from or near Ashby's Gap to John Gibson's Mill and from thence into the Road leading to Alexandria and that they Report to the Court the Conveniencies and inconveniencies that may attend the same

Test
Chas Binns Clerk

Loudoun

December Court 1773

Ordered that Thomson Ma____ Esq. John Lewis and William Brookes or any two (being first duly Qualified before some Magistrate for the County aforesaid) View the way for a Road to be opened from Mahlon Janney's Mill, across the Kittockton Mountain by William Cavin's Plantation into the Main Road leading from Nolands Ferry to Leesburg and that they make Report thereof to the Court of the conveniencies and inconveniencies that may attend the same being opened.

      Test
        Cha's Binns ClCur

Sworn
  Craven Peyton

(over)

  In obedience to the within Order we the Subscribers have Viewed the within mentioned Road &c. We judge a convenient Road may be had from the Quaker Meeting House on the Line between Wm Schooley's Land & Land that Wm Morrison lives on some distance then across a Corner of Wm Schooley's Land thence on the Line between F. Schooley's Land & Joseph Caldwell's then between s^d Caldwell's Land & Wm Cavin's thence along an old Road till it comes to a line between Mr Mason's & Mr Page's Land thence to the s^d Ferry Road

        John Lewis
        William Brookes

____ Ret^d &
____ to be Established
____ 1774
____ Cavins Over
____ Hamilton to
____ the Hands

Road Case File # 46   1774
Loudoun County Circuit Court
Leesburg, Virginia

December Court 1773

Ordered that Thompson Ma__ Esq. John Lewis and William Bronaugh or any two (being first duly Qualified before some Magistrate for the County aforesaid) View the way for a Road to be Opened from Mahlon Janney's Mill, across the Kittockton Mountain by William Cavin's Plantation into the main Road Leading from Nolands Ferry to Leesburg and that they make Report thereof to the Court of the Conveniences and inconveniencies that may attend the same being opened

Teste
Cha S Binns D Clk Cur

Sworn

To the Worshifull Court of Loudoun

Gentlemen

We your Petitioners humbly showeth that we labour under great difficulty for want of a Road leading f___ Mahlon Janneys Mill through our Settlement. We therefore Pray your Worships to Order a Road to be laid out & opened through our Settlement the most convenient & best way to said Mill.

William Woollard	William Cavins
Thomas Beavers	
Jacob Wells	
John Colwell	
Adam Carnahan	
William Gregg	
Joseph Megeach	
James Roch	
Mathew Hyinman	
John Humphreys	Jno Steere
Thomas Stevens	Ja^s Jones
Isaac Schawen	Jno Todhunter
Joseph Steere	Joseph Coleman
Joseph Calwell	
William Brookes	
Henry Oxley Junr	
James Stevens	
Wm Molton	

(over)

Wm Cavins Pet^o

1774 March 11, O^r that
Jno Steere, Ja^s Jones, John
Todhunter & Joseph
Coleman View the way
and Report.

Road Case File # 46   1774
Loudoun County Circuit Court
Leesburg, Virginia

To the Worshipfull Court of Loudoun
Gentlemen

As your petitioners Humbly sheweth that we
labour under great difficulty for want of a Road leading to
Mathew Tanners Mill though our will ment We therefore
pray your Worships to order a Road to be laid out & from henry
our settlement the most convenient of Carbing to said Mill

William Wodllard
Thomas Bevin
Jacob W___
John Colwell
Adam Carnahan
William Gregg
Joseph Megeach
Jones Roach
Mathew Hyneman
John Humphreys
Thomas Stevens
Isaac Dehaven
Joseph Peric
Joseph Calwell
William Brooks
Henry Oxley Jr
James Stevens
Wm Wotton

William Cavins

In there
Sal Jones
Sal Hochunter
Joseph Coleman

March the 10 Day 1774

By virtue of an Order of Loudoun County Court
We T. Owsley J. Lous and Wm. Robnson being first
Sworn have Viewed the most convenient way for a Road
from the County Line to John Gipsons Mill and from
the Mill to the Road. In our opinion from the Line
to Luwis Simons with a straight course thence to
T. Wests thence some to a new House as straight as
convenience suits thence to a Field that was Danils
Sons the best way is to (go) through but may go of
I hear said thence to Abram Lewis to go betwixt the
mider dan House with the least damage likewise by
Pal Lechus thence to the Mill thence to the under
Gipsons Land and crossing the Branch through a Corner
of his Field to the Alexsander Road to do the least
damage and be the best way.

        Thos. Owsley

        James Lewis

        William Robinson

(over)

Report of John
Gibson's Road
1774 March 14 Estab.
per Report Th^s West is
app^d Surveyor & W^m
Smith G^t to allot
the Hands.

Road Case File # 46   1774
Loudoun County Circuit Court
Leesburg, Virginia

March the 10 Day 1774 Loudoun County Cort
by varty of a order of Loudoun County Cort
we T. Ousby J. Lewis and Wm Robertson been first
haveing to find the most convenest way for a rod from the
County line to John Gipsons mill and from the
mill to the rod in order[?] now[?] from the
Lin to Lewis demons with a Strait Cost thence
to T. ____ thence one to a new house as it be as
as can run one street thence to a field that
was Daniels Son the best to near yett to throw th
__ may for a Sheep __ thence to Abram Lewis
to go between them, Jordans house with the best James
__ ____ pal Leehy thence to the mill
thence to the wider Gipsons Cornan
crosen the branch then with a corner
of his feld to the ____ ____ to
do the best Jurnuey and be the best way

Thos. Ousbey
James Lewis
William Johnson

To the Worshipful Court of Loudoun now sitting in
Leesburg in and for the said County_____
The Petition of us the Subscribers
                                    Humbly showeth
that your Worships was pleased at your last Session
to Order Viewers on a Road at the request of William
Cavins to be laid on the Line betwixt Joseph Colwell
and William Schooley & on the Line betwixt said
Schooley and William Morrison which Lands will be
Ja^s Ball he being Heir at Law, and on the Line betwixt
Francis Hague and Wm Schooley into the Main Great Road
leading from Mr. Knowland Ferry to Malon Jannys Mill.
And your Worships Petitioners have seen that the said
Viewers hath not regarded your Worships Order, but
hath contrary thereto Viewed the Lands of Wm Schooley
for said Road to be laid on, and hath also cut of a
part of said Francis Hagues Land which View is tending
greatly to damage each of your Worships Petitioners.
Said View also exempts Mr Colwells Lands being in the
least affected, although said Road is entirely for the
benefit of Mr Cavin and Mr Colwell wherefore your
Worships Petitioners Prays redress in said Case and
we as in duty bound shall pray.

            William Schooley
            Francis Hague
            James Ball

(over)

Schooley & c.
for Road
_____
April 1774

Road Case File # 46   1774
Loudoun County Circuit Court
Leesburg, Virginia

To [the Worshipful] Court of [Loudoun, a Court] in
Leesburg in and for the said County
the petition of us the subscribers

Humbly sheweth
that whereas your worships was pleas'd at your last sesion
To order Vewers on a Roade at the request of William Cavins
To be laid on the line betwixt Joseph Colwell and William
Schooley & on the line betwixt Said Scholey and William
Morrison which Lands Will be Jas Ball he Being Heir at Law
And on the line Betwixt francis Hague and Wm Schooley into
the Main great Rode Leading from [   ] Knowland ferry to
Malon Janny's Mill, And your Worships Petetioners have
seen that the Said Vewers haith Not Regarded your
Worships order But haith Contrary thereto Vewed the
Lands of Wm Schooley for Said Road to be laid on,
and have also Cut of a part of Said francis Hagues Land
Which Veiw is Tending greatly to Damage Each of your
Worships Petetioners, Said Vew also Exempts Mr Colwells
Lands being in the Least Affected Altho Said Road is
Intirely for the Benifit of Mr Cavin and Mr Colwell
Wherefore your Worships Petetioners Prays Redress
in Said Case and we as in Duty Bound Shall
Pray
William Schooley
Francis Hague
James Ball

Loudoun Sct   April Court 1774

Ordered that John Cavins James Best & Nathan Laycock or any two (being first duly Qualified before some Magistrate for this County) so View the most convenient way for turning a Road round Col. James Hamiltons Field, and make their Report of the conveniencies & inconveniencies that may attend the same.

                 Test Cha's Binns Cl.Court

(over)

Pursuant to the within Order we the Subscribers hath Viewed the Road within mentioned and find that the way we have marked out will be a better way and nearer &c. Certify under our hands this 10th day of May 1774.

                 John Cavins
                 Nathan Laycock

I hereby Certify that the above persons have Sworn before   Jas Hamilton

Road Case File # 46   1774
Loudoun County Circuit Court
Leesburg, Virginia

Pursuant to the within order I have caused the within named Stephen Tubbs who hath sworn he Road is of the whole sum I find that he is way we have marked as it will be added to my and I have order and one hundred his 10 lb charge this day of 1774

Joseph Ellis
Chase Lippincott

I hereby certify that the above named persons were sworn before

Ja Hammons

L_____n to wit   September_____ 1774

Ordered that Isaac Vanbuskirk, Joh_ Vanbuskirk, Adam Shover and William Shover or any three of them (being first duly Qualified before some Magistrate for this County) do View the way for a Road to lead from George Bowlings between Peter Millers & Daniel Michaels to John Georges Mill & Report to the Court the conveniencies & inconveniencies that may attend the same.

                 Teste Cha's Binns Cl Cur

(over)

Isaac Vanbuskirk Sworn by William Douglass
               Sept. 18, 1774

S C   _____Vanbuskirk & others to View Road

(not legible or decipherable)

Road Case File # 46   1774
Loudoun County Circuit Court
Leesburg, Virginia

Loudoun Sct   August Court 1774

    Ordered that Pearce Bailey, Joseph Bailey, William Robinson and William Rust or any three who being first duly Qualified according to Law do View the most convenient way for a Road to be cleared from Thomas Drakes Meadow to Leven Powell's Mill and make Report thereof to the Court of the conveniencies and inconveniencies that may attend the same.

        Test   Cha's Binns Cl. Cur.

In obedience to the above Order we the Subscribers being first Sworn before Thos Lewis Gent have viewed the way from Thos Drakes Meadow to Levin Powells Mill as therein directed, and that we do think the most convenient way for a Road is as follows Viz. To go from the said Drakes Meadow along the old way to Dawson Brown's Plantation & through a Corner of his Wheat Field thence across the Beaver Dam along the old way by Capt. William Bronaugh and William ___ith Gent. and Simon Hancks, thence across the Road leading from Ashbys Gap to Abslom Rameys with a straight line to strike the Road that leads from the Ford of Goose Creek to the Land of Mr Owsley where the said Owsley has a Still House thence along the said Road until it meets the Road leading from Ashbys Gap to Mr Powells.

                Peirce Bayly
                Joseph Bayly
                William Robinson

(over)

Loudoun Sct
    The within named Pearce Bayley, Joseph Bayley, & William Robinson, duly qualified this 30th of Sept 1774, Before
                Thos Lewis

P. Bailey
Jo. Bailey
W. Robinson
W. Rust   Report of a Road
to View Road

Report of a Road   1774 October 10th
Aug. 11th 1774   Established Thomas
                              Owsley Ovr Thos
―――――――――   Lewis to allot hands

Established & Overr appointed

Loudoun ss.   August Court 1774

Ordered that Pearce Bailey, Joseph Bailey
William Robinson and William Bush, or
any three of them being first duly Qualified
according to Law do View the most Con
:venient way for a Road to be cleared
from Thomas Drakes Meadow to Leven
Powells Mill and make Report thereof to the
Court of the Conveniences and Inconvenien
:cies that may attend the same.

             Tost Ch. Binns Clk

In Obedience to the above order we the Subscribers
being first Sworn before Thos Lewis Gent. have viewed
the way from Thomas Drakes Meadow to Leven Powells Mill
as therein Directed, And we do think the most Convenient
way for a Road is as follows Vizt. to go from the said
Drakes Meadow along the Old way to Dawson
Browns Plantation & through a Corner of his Wheatfield
Thence a[long] the Beaver Dam along the Old way by Capt
William Binaugh and between William [Sm]ith Gent and
Simon Hancks, Thence a[cross] the Road Le[ad]ing from Ashbys
Gap to Absolom Rameys with a Straight Line to Strike the
Road that Do from the fork of Goosecreek [to] the Land of
Mr Owsley, here the said Owsley has [built] a Mill House
Thence along the said Road untill it M[eets] the Road
Leading from Ashbys Gab to Mr Powells.

             Peirce Bayly
             Joseph Bayly
             William Robinson

To the Worshipful Court of Loudoun County
We have laid out the Road to the best advantage and
least damage to the water & Land and it is to run
from where the Road comes down from Gorge Bollin
Drain to the Quarter Branch up the Quarter Branch
til to Peter Millers then between Peter Miller and
Dan Mikel til the corner of Peter Millers Field a-new
that in a straight line til to a Dam for a Drain
a round in the Road that comes from (?) (?)
from that to John Gorgs Mill.

   Henry Cime   Isaac Vanbuskirk
   (?) (?) for over   John Vanbuskirk
   seas   Adam Shover

(over)

Report of a
Road
Oct. 11th 1774
Established

Christr Greenup

Christr Greenup

Road Case File # 46   1774
Loudoun County Circuit Court
Leesburg, Virginia

To the onnorabell Court of Pleadair

Gam Iyour Greas Peatient the Poor to the
Poor advantage and large Damamgees the
Art and Marr and at its to Come rehair
the Pe Pers Doues some gorge Betler Duarto
the spart speally the quit Beter that to
Plum Keigs that his Contrey understands
iiy hach the Cornsaaghtes under nond Pas
that am have the t: Pauill of a aldeaces
spradinthe Pear that Couse ima forg deat
lieu thatis Johns 1799 and Sagem Enghats
Henman Cine Duncan Eyhauf
of Ban letc perctoas

Dum Norca

Miscellaneous Road Cases File No. 47, 1778
Clerk of Circuit Court
Archives
Leesburg, Virginia

Loudoun Sct

In obedience to an Order of the Worshipfull Court of Loudoun County We the Subscribers have viewed the way for a Road from Mr George Nixons Mill to the Main Road at Houghs Mill, do make the following report.

From the said Mill to go along the Road lead^g by Abraham Hugulys, straightening the same where convenient, until it comes to the farther corner of the said Hugulys Fence, thence thro' a piece of woods, nearly as there is some slight marks made, until it intersects the said Road again then keeping the said Road to a marked hickory, then turning to the right & keep^g along a Ridge as the same is lately marked until it comes into Vestals Gap Road just where the Road turns out to Wm Meads & we can't conceive the said Road will be of prejudice to any person.

Given under our hands
this 9th day of Decr 1778

Christ^o Greenup
John Cotton
John Jones

(over)

Report of a Road
from Nixon's Mill
to the Road by Saml
Hough's Mill

1778 Decr 14th Est.
Abraham Huguly Overseer
J. Alex' to allot the Hands

Road Case File # 47 1778
Loudoun County Circuit Court
Leesburg, Virginia

Loudoun ss.

In Obedience to an Order of the Worshipfull Court of Loudoun County We the subscribers have viewed the way for a Road from Mr George Nixon's Mill to the Main Road at Hough's Mill, do make the following report

From the said Mill to go along the road leading by Abraham Hugely's Straightning the same where convenient until it comes to the farther corner of the said Hugely's fence, thence thro' a piece of Woods nearly as there is some slight marks made, until it intersects the said Road again then keeping the said Road to a marked Hickory then turning to the right & keeping along a ridge as the same is lately marked until it comes into Vestals Gap Road just where the Road turns out to Wm Mead's & We can't conceive the said Road will be of any prejudice to any Person Given under our hands this 9th day of Decr 1778

Christo Greenup
John Price
John Price

In obedience to an Order of the Worshipful
Court of Loudoun We the Subscribers have viewed the
way from George Nixons Mill to Wm Houghs Mill,
report as follows. From the said Nixons Mill along
the Lane until it intersects s^d Nixons Line between
s^d Nixon & Lee, then with said Line thro' a Corner
of Stephen Morlans Field until it comes into the old
Road leading down by the Saw Mill then along the Road
to Jones Road, then along that Road to the Carolina
Road, then near the Line between Binns & Mead. Still
continued on the Line or near between Wren & Harbour,
then along an old Road leading by Lafevers straight
the same the best way to said Houghs Mill & we think
the same will be of no prejudice to any person.

        John Cotton
        Christ^o Greenup
        John Jones

(over)

Report of Road
from Nixons Mill
to Houghs Mill

1778 Decr 14th
Est. P. Harbour Ov^r
J. Alexander to allot
the Hands

Road Case File # 47   1778
Loudoun County Circuit Court
Leesburg, Virginia

In obedience to an Order of the Worshipful Court of Loudoun We the subscribers have viewed the way from George Nixons Mill to W.m Houghs Mill. Report as follows. From the said Nixons Mill along the lane until it intersects S.d Nixon's line, between S.d Nixon & Lee, then with said line thro' a corner of Stephen Morlans field until it comes into the old Road leading down by the Saw Mill then along that Road to Jones Road then along that Road to the Carolina Road, then on the line between Binns & Mead, still continued on the line or near between Wren & Harbour, then along an Old Road leading by Lafevers straight the same the best way to said Houghs Mill & we think the same will be of no prejudice to any Person.

John Sutton
Christo Greenup
John Jones

183

Miscellaneous Road Cases File No. 48, 1780 to 1782
Clerk of Circuit Court
Archives
Leesburg, Virginia

Agreeable to an Order of April Court we have Reviewed
Isemans Mill Road, beginning in Gallahans Road near
Peter Grahams thence through said Grahams Field
to said Isemans Mill thence up the Mill Race to the
Creek above the Mill Dam then cross the Creek and up
the Hill to the Corner of Jonas Bradleys Field
thence through the Field a pretty straight course in to
the Millstone Road opposite said Bradleys Spring House.

May 6th 1780   Jonathan Conrad
                                 John Conrad
                                 John Wolf

(over)

Report of Iser-
mans Road

1780 May 8th
retd & Established
John Conrad Ovr

Road Case File # 48   1780-1782
Loudoun County Circuit Court
Leesburg, Virginia

agreable to an order of April Court we have Reviewed
Gesmans mill Road, Begining in gallahans Road near
peter Grahams thence through Said Grahams field
to Said Gesmans mill thence up the mill Race to the
Creek above the mill Dam then Cross the Creek and up
the hill to the Corner of Jonas Bradleys field
thence through the field a pretty Strait Course, to
the millstone Road opposite Bradleys Spring house

may 6th 1780

Jonathan Conrad
John Conrad
John Wolf

Loudoun Sct   April Court   1780

Ordered that Thomas Shores, Nathanial Smith, William Fields and John McClain or any three of them being first Sworn do View the way for turning the Carolina Road as proposed by William McClellan and report to the Court the conveniencies and inconveniencies that may attend the same.

Test   Cha's Binns Cl Cour

(over)

In obedience to the within Order We the Subscribers being first Sworn have Viewed the Way as Directed by William McClan and allow it more convenient and better than the old Way as Witness our hands.

Wm Field
John McClain
Nathanial Smith

(over)

Order & return
of M^r McClellans
   Road
1780 May 8
established

Road Case File #48   1780-1782
Loudoun County Circuit Court
Leesburg, Virginia

Loudoun [to wit?] April Court 1789

Ordered that Thomas Shores, Nathanuel Smith, William Beech and John McLain or any three of them being first sworn do view the way for turning the road heretofore [by] William McClellan Caroline and report to the Court the conveniencies and inconveniencies that may attend the same.

Test. Cha's Binns D.Clk

In obedience to the Within order We the Subscribers being first Sworn Have Vewed the Way as Directed By William McClain and Allow it More Convenient or Better than the Old Way as witness our hand

W'm Tr[...]
John McL[...]
Nathan'l [...]

7th June 1780

We the Subscribers being first Sworn agreeable to the Order of Court to Review a Road from Shugarland Meeting House to Mr John Dowdles Mill.

Beginning at the Meeting House running thence between John Grens & Charnick Selfs thence along a Ridge near the old Mill Path to the Road that leads from Broad Run to said MIll then from said Mill cross a small Branch then along a Ridge between Jacob Hieugley & Jobe Hiegley to Trammells Rolling Road then along the said Road to a Glade called (?) Hickrey then along a Ridge the Upper Side of Mathew White to the Mine Branch crossing the said Branch to the said Road leading from Leesburg to Alexandria at the top of Difficult Hill.

   Richd Valandingham Samson Tramell & Spensor Wigington

(over)

Report of John
Dowdalls Mill
   Road
_____

1780 June 12th Est.
Smith King Overs.

Road Case File # 48   1780-1782
Loudoun County Circuit Court
Leesburg, Virginia

4th June 1788

We the Subscribers being first sworn agreeable to the
Order of Court to View a road from Augusta
Meeting house to Mr. John Douglas Mill

Begining at the Meeting house Running thence
Between John Greers & Thomas Diggs thence along
a Ridge to D. Mill hath to the Road that Leads
from Broad Run to Said mill thence on Said Hill
to a small Branch then along an Dig Between
Jos. Beverleys & Jo. Kirkleys to Samuell Rodins
Gate then along the Said Road to a Glade Leaving
Jos. Kirkerys then along a Ridg the other Side of
the Glade then past the mine Branch Birghts the Said
Beverleys to the Said Road Leading from Leesburg to
Dikes Va, ... ghan Camos Isaacs & Thomas Biging [torn]

189

April the 29th 1780

Agreeable to an Order of the worshipfull Court of Loudoun we the subscriber being first sworn have viewed the Road from the Road near Thos Greggs to Col. Triplets Mill and begins as follows. Near the Lane between Isaac Bodines and where Willets lived from thence to the upper Corner of the Widow Combses Field thence along the said Field to the next Corner thence down to Thos Mounts and thence to Robert McCullys Tan-house thence to the old Ford on the Beaver Dam thence with the old Road to James Mahonnahs Fence thence with the said Fence to the Leesburg Road and cross the said Road to the County Road thence with the said Road to the Mill the Road is to continue with Mahonahs Fence till he gets (?) crop of corn then to go with the Line between the said Mahonah and Francis Triplets.

            John Taylor
            Richard Crupper
            Thos Gregg

(over)

Report of Tripletts
Mill Road

1780 June 12th
retd Tho. Mount Ovr
S. Triplett to allot
the hands

Road Case File # 48   1780-1782
Loudoun County Circuit Court
Leesburg, Virginia

April the 29th 1780

Agreeable to an order of the worshipfull Court of Loudoun we the subscribers being first sworn have vewed the Road from the Road near Thos. Greggs to Col. Triplets Mill and begens at ~~a hollow~~ near the Lane between Isaac Bodines and where Willets lived from thence to the upper corner of the widow Combses field thence along the said field to the next corner thence down to Thos. Mounts and thence to Robert McCullys Tan house thence to the old ford on the Beaverdam thence with the old Road to James Mahonnahs fence thence with the said fence to the Leesburg Road and cross the said Road to the County Road thence with the said Road to the Mill, the Road is to continue with Mahonahs fence till he gets of Crop of Corn then to go with the line between the said Mahonah and Francis Triplets

John Taylor
Richard Cruppe
Thos Gregg

Loudoun Sct   June Court 1780

Ordered that Benjamin Cockerile, Sandford Cockerile, John Whaley & John Curtis or any three of them being first duly Sworn do view the way for turning the Ox Road as proposed by Wethers Smith & make report to the Court of the conveniencies & inconveniencies that may attend the same.

                    Test
                        Cha's Binns Cl Cur

(over)

Agreeable to the within Order We the Subscribers have Viewed the way for turning the Ox Road as Propos'd by Weathers Smith and in our opinion it may be easily made a better Road & think it will be something nearer as Witness our hands this 29th day of June 1780.

                Sanford Cockerill
                John Whaley
                Benj. Cockerill

Loudoun Sct Sandford Cockerill & Benj. Cockerill Sworn before H. Lane
                    26th June 1780

John Whaley Sworn before Har. Lane
                    June 29th 1780

Order View
Smith's Road

1780 Augt 14th
Established

Road Case File # 48   1780 - 1782
Loudoun County Circuit Court
Leesburg, Virginia

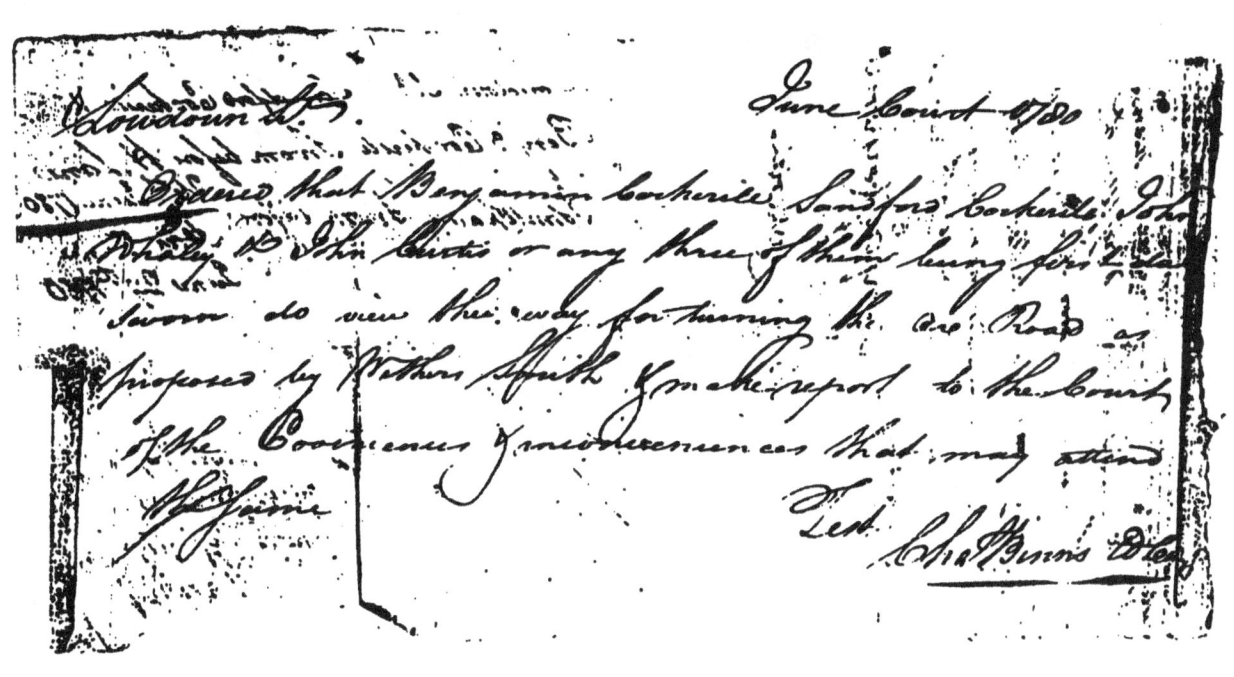

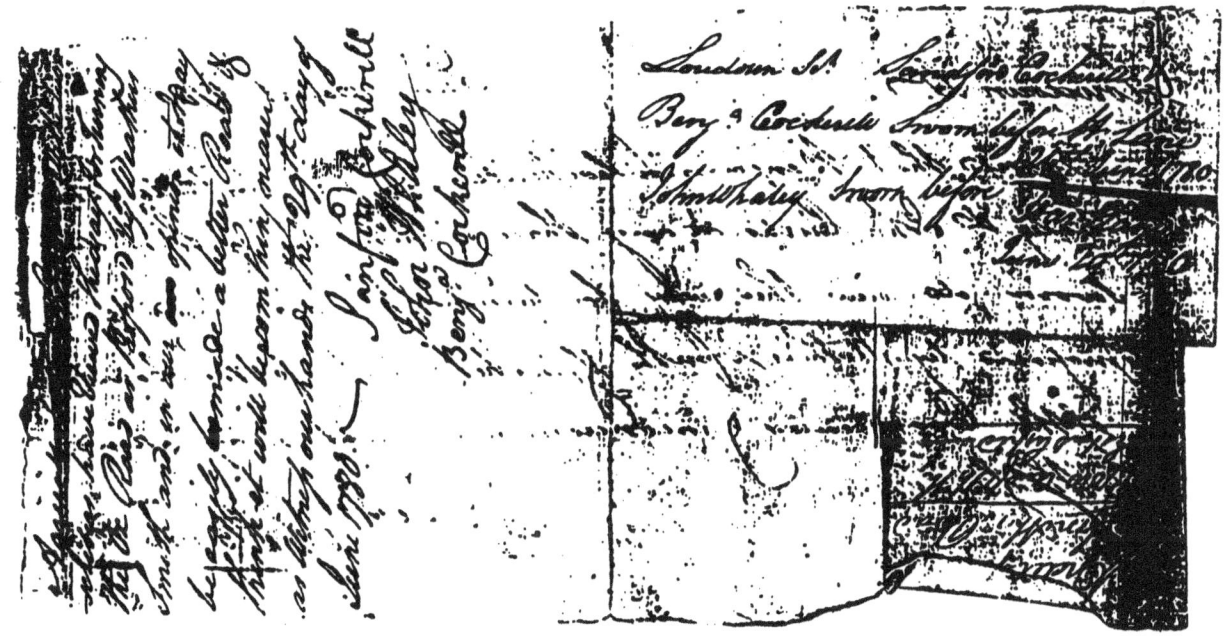

In obedience to an Order of the Worshipful Court of Loudoun We the Subscribers being first Sworn have Viewed a way for a Road leading from Colonel Simon Tripletts Mill to an old Road nigh to David Rees Blacksmith's Shop are as followeth Viz. Beginning at the Ford of Goose Creek at the Mouth of the Mill Branch and up the said Branch to an old Road then with the said Road about thirty Rod(s), and bearing to the right with the Path called Sanders Path then keeping near the said path to where James Sanders formerly lived thence through Bernard Van Horns Bottom Field to a Ford on Goose Creek a little above the said Field thence with the Path to Jonathan Tools House thence nigh M:r Thaddeus MacCartys House thence to the Line between M:r Joseph Farrows old Place and Henry Battertons Plantation thence with the said Line with a direct course to the Mouth of Joseph Farrows Lane thence with a direct course to an old Road where Hails Road intersects   Dated September the fifth Day One Thousand Seven Hundred and Eighty_____ 1780_____

         Richard Crupper
         Thaddeus MiCarty
         John Walker

(over)

Report of a Road
from S. Tripletts
Mill

1780 Sept:r 11 ret:d &
estab. Aram Hagerman
Overseer & Hands all:d

Road Case File # 48   1780-1782
Loudoun County Circuit Court
Leesburg, Virginia

In Obedience to an Order of the Worshipful Court of Loudoun We the Subscribers being first Sworn have Viewed a Way or a Road leading from Colonel Simon Triplett's Mill to and of a which to David Rees Blacksmith Shop are an follows to wit Beginning at the End of Goose Creek at the mouth of the little Branch and up the said Branch to an Old Road then with the said Road about thirty Rod, and bearing to the right with the Path called Vardens Path, then keeping near the said Path to where James Sanders formerly lived thence through Bernard Van Horns Bottom fields a Yard on Goose Creek a little above the said Field thence with the Path to Jonathan Tools thence Nigh Mr Thaddeus Mac Cartys Hough thence to the line between Mr Josiah Tarrours & Stone and Henry Ballentines Plantation thence with the said with a Direct Course to the Mouth of Josiah Tarrours Lane hence with a Direct Course to an Old Road where Hall Road intersects Dated September the fifth Day One thousand seven hundred and Eighty — 1700 —

Richard Bruyneer
Gardener Whorton
Jor m walker

Loudoun Sct   August Court 1780

    Ordered that James Coleman Robert Frier and William Stanhope Gentlemen or any two of them be appointed Commissioners from this County to meet the Commissioners of Fairfax County to view Difficult Bridge and report whether they think the same sufficiently performed per agreement, and also that they take the number of Tithables in order to ascertain the proportion to be paid by this County.

        Teste   Cha's Binns Cl Cur

The number of Tithables
returned for Loudoun County
in 1779 is 3,075
        Ch. Binns CC

Fairfax County 2,673 Tithables in 1779

(over)

In obedience to the within Order We the Subscribers Commissioners from Loudoun & Fairfax Courts have Viewed Difficult Bridge and think the same sufficiently performed, and can not ascertain the proportion to be paid by the County for want of the number of Tithables in Fairfax County as Witness our hands the 26th Sept. 1780
        James Coleman
        Wm Stanhope
        J. Broadwater
        Jno Wren

For
Jas Coleman Gen.
& others to View
Difficult Bridge

1780 Nov. 13 Ord.
to be paid Viz.
₤ 853.5.6 by Loud.

Road Case File # 48   1780-1782
Loudoun County Circuit Court
Leesburg, Virginia

Loudoun [blotted] August Court 1780

Ordered [blotted] James Coleman Robert Frier and William [blotted] Gentlemen or any two of them be appointed Commissioners from this County to meet the Commissioners of Fairfax County to view Difficult bridge and report whether they think the same sufficiently performed as p Agreement, and also that they take the Number of Tithables in order to ascertain the proportion to be paid by this County

Teste Cha. Binns CClr

The number of Tithables returned for Loudoun County in 1779 is 3075

Ch. Binns C C

Fairfax County 2675 Tithables in 1779

Loudoun Sct   March Court 1781

On the Motion of Thompson Mason Esqr Ordered
that Wm Douglass, Thomas Respess & Joshua
Daniel Gt being first sworn do View the way
for turning the Main Road from James Cooks
House to the Quarter of the said Mason & make
Report thereof to the Court.

         Teste
            Cha's Binns Cl Cur

(over)

By virtue of the within Order we have
Viewed the Road & think the Road may be turned
near James Cookses by an Apple Tree from thence
below the Great Spring from thence in a straight
line to the Main Road may be done without
prejudice to any person.

                William Douglass
                Thomas Respas
                Joshua Daniel

                May '81 retd
                & estabd

Road Case File # 48   1780-1782
Loudoun County Circuit Court
Leesburg, Virginia

Loudoun Sc't   At a March Court 1794

On the motion of Thompson Mason Esq'r Ordered
that M'r Douglass Thomas Respess William
Daniel &ct being first sworn do view the Way
for turning the Main Road from James Cooks
House to the Quarter of the said Mason & make
Report thereof to the Court as ...

                                                Teste
                                        Cha's Binns D. Clerk

By Virtue of the within Order we have
viewed the said ... the Road may be turned
... James Cooks ... a pine tree ...
thence below the ... thence in a
straight line ... new Road may be ...
without prejudice to any person ...
                                        William Douglass
                                        Thomas Respess
                                        Joshua Daniel
                                        ...

Loudoun County Sct   October Court 1781

    Ordered that James McGeeith, Stephen Roszell, Thos Gregg and Joshua Dunkin or any three of them being first Sworn or Affirmed before some Justice of the Peace for this County do view the Way for a Road from Thomas Garrett's at the Mountain Road to Joseph Janney's Mill and Report the conveniencies & inconveniencies that may attend the same to the Court.

                        Teste Cha's Binns Cl cur

(over)

Agreeable to the within Order, we have Viewed the Way and Report as follows Viz. To run from the Mountain Road upon the Line between Garret & Nichols till it comes into Canbeys Road, then along s^d Road to the foot of a Hill opposit Thos Griggs Meadow, then along the side of the Hill to Ben. Clearys Land then through his Wood Land down to Janneys Mill. Given under our hands this 6th Day of June 1782.

                      James Megeath
                      Joshua Duncan
                      Stephen Roszel

Order for View Road

June 1782 Ret^d
& Established

Road Case File # 48 1780-1782
Loudoun County Circuit Court
Leesburg, Virginia

October Court 1781

Ordered that James McGeach Stephen Rossell [...] Duncan or any three of them being first sworn or affirmed before some Justice of the Peace for this County to view the Way for a Road from [...] to the Mountain Road to Joseph [Janney's Mill] and report the Conveniences & Inconveniences [...] the same to the Court
Teste
Cha[s] Binns C[lk]

Loudoun County

By virtue of an Order from the worshipfull the Court of the County aforesaid to us directed we being first Sworn have viewed the Road leading from Mr Benj^a Edwards to Leesburg and are of opinion that the Road shall go as it now does from Benj^a Edwards to a pole Bridge thence in a straight line to a Gate that stands in the Ferry Road from thence as the Road now is to Leesburg which we think cannot prejudice any person. Given under hands June 11, 1782.

                                  William Douglass
                                  John Lewis
                                  Thos Respess

(over)

B. Edwards Road
Estab. June '82

Road Case File # 48   1780-1782
Loudoun County Circuit Court
Leesburg, Virginia

Loudoun County

The Court of this County, exposcaid to we alterd forbearing
fiel Sworn, have reviewed the road leading from Mr Berry's
Edwards to Leesburg and are of opinion that the
road shall go as it now does from Berry's Edwards to
a pole bridge thence in a streight line to the gap that
leads to the ferry, and from thence both the road now
to Leesburg which we think cannot Prejudice
any Person. Given Under hand June 11 1792

William Douglass
John Littlejohn
[signature]

Pursuant to an Order of the County Court of Loudoun We the Subscribers named in the said Order being first Sworn have Viewed the way which Joseph Lacey proposes to turn the Road, leading from Coxes Mill to the Prince William Line & do Report as follows. To turn out of the present Road at a Path on the West Side near the Ford of Goose Creek, then running with or near the said Path through Ellzeys Land then with the said Path through Ellzeys Land by Stadlers House to a Dividing Line between Ellzey & Carter showed us by Majr Saml Cox, then running with or near the said Dividing Line between the said Ellzey & Carter to Majr Charles Wests Land, then running with or near a Dividing Line between the said West & Carter to Thomas Floods land, then running with or near a Dividing Line between the said Flood & Carter to or near a White Oak Carters Corner on or near Owsleys Branch, then nearly the same course continued through the Plantation of the said Joseph Lacey which he purchased from John Hall about ten or fifteen pole(s) to the westward of the dwelling Houses, still continuing nearly the same course through the said Laceys Plantation about two or three pole(s) to the eastward of a White Oak Corner between John Moore & the said lacey, then slanting through Laceys Land to the Line dividing him & Moore then with their Dividing Line & after the termination of Moores Land, then by a Dividing Line between Majr Charles West & the said lacey to Capt Thomas Wests Land, then continuing nearly the same course through a small Corner of the said Thomas Wests Land until it intersects the present Road in a broad Lane between the said Charles & Thomas West. We are of opinion that the land over which the intended Road is to pass will be nearer & on higher & dryer ground the greater part of the way than the present Road, and running on the Dividing Lines. Except where it runs through Coxes land to Ellzeys land also then on Ellzeys Land to Carters Line near Stadlers House also through Laceys Land to Moores Line & through a small corner of Capt Thomas Wests Land.

(over)

Given under our hands this 8th day of August 1782

Report of Road
Peto for by J. Lacey
1782 Aug 12th
heard and set aside

Jas Davis
Jn. Tyler
John Smarr
John Hall

Ch. Greenup
Col. Triplet
Thos (?)
Dan Feagan
John Jones

Road Case File # 48   1780-1782
Loudoun County Circuit Court
Leesburg, Virginia

Pursuant to an Order of the County Court of Loudoun We the subscribers named in the said Order being first sworn have Viewed the way which Joseph Lacey proposes to turn the road leading from Lewis Mill to the Prince William line & do report as follows. To turn out of the present road at a path on the West side near the ford of Goose Creek, then running with or near the said path through Ellzey's land by Stadler's house to a dividing line between Ellzey & Carter shewed us by Majr. Sam'l Cox. then running with or near the said dividing line between the said Ellzey & Carter to Majr. Charles West's land, then running with or near a dividing line between the said West & Carter to Thomas Flood's land, then running with or near a dividing line between the said Flood & Carter to or near a White Oak Carter's corner on or near Cowleys branch, then nearly the same course continued through the plantation of the said Joseph Lacey which he purchased from John Wall about ten or fifteen pole to the Westward of the dwelling houses, still continuing nearly the same course through the said Lacey's plantation about two or three pole to the Eastward of a White Oak corner between John Moss & the said Lacey, then slanting through Lacey's land this including him & Moss then with their dividing line after the termination of Moss's land, then by a dividing line between Majr. Charles West & the said Lacey to to Capt. Thomas West's land, then continuing nearly the same course through a small corner of the said Thomas West's land untill it intersects the present road in a broad lane between the said Charles & Thomas West, We are of Opinion that the land over which the intended road is to pass will be nearer & on higher & dryer ground the greater part of the way than the present road — And turning on the dividing lines except where it runs through Ellzey's land to Carter's line near Stadler's where also through Lacey's land to Moss's line & through a small corner of Capt. Thomas West's land

To the Worshipfull The Court of Loudoun

The Petition of Peter Carr & sundry of his Neighbors humbly showeth that the Main Road as it now stands leading from Leesburg to Winchester might be made much leveler and as near to be taken and under the Hill where the old Road formerly went and so along just a little below the House of Peter Carr in a straight line to the Main Road by John Williams and Pray a Survey may be got on the same and your Petitioners as in duty bound shall Pray & c.

       Peter Carr
       George Neafus
       John Dodd
       John Orisson
       Richard Wattson

(over)

Pet^n for a Road

Order of View
Granted Sept^r
 1782

Road Case File # 48 1780-1782
Loudoun County Circuit Court
Leesburg, Virginia

To The Worshipfull The Court of Loudoun

The Petition of Peter Carr & Sundry of his Neighbours Humbly Sheweth That The main road as it now Stands Leading from Leesburg to Winchester might be made much Beteller and as near to be taken out under the Hill Where the old road formerly went — and to along Just a little below the house of Petr Carr in a Streight Line to the main road by John Milhounoux and Pray a Survey may be Gott on the Sd and your petitioners &c

Pray &c —

Peter Carr
George Beaton
John Carter
Cha Orrison
Richard Wattson

Loudoun County Sct.   Sepr Court 1782

   Ordered that John Dodd Wm Roberts James Claypole
& Hamilton Rogers or any three of them being first
Qualified as the Law directs before some Justice of
the Peace for the said County do view the most
convenient way for turning the Main Road leading from
Leesburg to Winchester on the motion of Peter Carr &
return their Report to Court.

               Tete   Cha's Binns Cl. Cur

(over)

          Mr Peter Carr

Loudoun Sc.   Agreeable to the within Order I have
Qualified John Dodd William Roberts & James Claypoole
to view the within mentioned Road & so make a Return
to the Court. Given from under my this 13 Day of
Octr 1782.

                John Alexander

Road Case File # 48   1780-1782
Loudoun County Circuit Court
Leesburg, Virginia

Loudoun County ss. Sept. Court 1782

Ordered that John Dodd, Wm. Roberts, James Claypole & Hamilton Rogers or any three of them being first qualified as the law directs before some Justice of the Peace for the said County do view the most convenient way for turning the Waggon Road leading from Leesburg to Winchester on the motion of Peter Carr & return their Report to —

Teste Chas Binns ClCur

Mr. Peter Carr

Loudoun ss. Agreeable to the within Order, James Claypole, John Dodd, William Roberts ... the within mentioned ... to make a return ...
Given from under my hand this 19 day of Oct. 1782

John Alexander

To the Worshipful Court of Loudoun County We your
Petitioners humbly showeth that we are fully convinced
from our acquaintance with the Road leading from Doutys
to Leesburgh would be much to the advantage of Peter
Carr and no disadvantage to any individual more than
where it now goes if it should be continued by the said
Carrs Dwelling-house where it formerly went for many years
and whereas there has been a Review and Report to continue
it where it now is we are of opinion that the Viewers was
not acquainted with all circumstances we therefore pray
that a Review upon the said Road may be appointed.

Thomas Gest	Peter Harbart	John Neilson
Isaac Nichols	Elisha Marks	Israel Pancoast
John James	Thomas Hague	Griffy Perce
George Neafus	William Mourhead	Thomas Adams
Farling Ball	Thomas Rodgers	John Bishop
Andrew Smith	Peter Hunsman	Joseph Caldwell
And^w Ireland	James Craig	Moses Caldwell
Josiah White Jun.	George Nixon	John Caldwell
	Joseph Wilson	John Adams
	George Squires	John Piet Sen
	Benjamin Woodley	Philip Edwards
	John March	Abraham Davis
	Richard Osburn	Thomas Humphreys
	John Truax	William Shreve
	Moses Thomas	James Best
	John Smith	Timothy Hixson
	Thos Marks	John Binns
	Wm Wildman	David Henry
	Nathan Lacock	John McGeach
	Jacob Wildman	John Henry Jun.

(over)

Review   Geo. Emery
         Ben. Shreeves
         Alex. MacMichins
         James Claypole
Carrs Pet. Road

Road Case File # 48   1780-1782
Loudoun County Circuit Court
Leesburg, Virginia

To the worshipfull Court of Loudoun County we your
Petitioners Humbly Sheweth that we are fully Convinced
from our acquaintance with the Road leading from Dou[g]h
-regory's road Leonard Hii: advantage of the Leesburg
To Leesburg is would be much to his advantage of the Leesburg
and no (Leaders Co is to any individual more than wheres
Now as Si: it is found by the said Loven Douch
any house whe it is formerly Contained by his said Coven Ouck
Whereas there has been a Petition pre- - - to Continue at
Where i: now is the way of Petition that it came up vp
Ho: acquainted with he act Convaying he Road to be
any that a frveas we hoop the can Convaying he Road

Thomas Kei[th] Peter Harbert   John Nilson
              Isaac Nichols   Israel Bancorn?
                 John Hague   Lurifif Peirce
     John Nichols William Hodges Thomas Jones
              George? Nealy?

Ralph Bell
David Smith
Angus McFarland
Joseph Hutchcraft
Joseph Whitesides
James Bare
George Bristoe
Christopher Holton
George Ogburn
Benjamin Woolly
John Neave
Richard Williams
David Dixon
Alfred Harris
John Smith
Thos. T. Clarke
Wm. S. Oldman
Nathaniel Henry
Jacob Thomas

Thomas Hodges
Moses Phenomen
Moses Bare
John Bristoe
John Adams
John Baxter
Philip Edwards
Abraham Price
Kinzea Stewart
William Bruce
James Bent
Timothy Hopper
John Burns
James Henry
John [illegible]
John Henry
John Cabinet
John Barnett

A
Acker, Peter 144
Adams, John 210
Adams, Thomas 210
Alex', J. 180
Alexander, J. 182
Alexander, John 152, 208
Alexandria 89, 118, 162, 188
Alexsanders road 168
Anderson, Cornelius 95, 97
Aruecosts, John, land 103
Ashbys Gap 39, 114, 162, 176
Aubery, Wm. 80
Awbrey, Thos. 80
Awbrey, Thos. ferry of 80
Awbrey, Thos. ferry boat of 80

B
Bailey, Jo. 176
Bailey, Joseph 176
Bailey, P. 176
Ball, Far. 132
Ball, Farlin 132
Ball, James 170
Ball, Jas. 170
Balls, Farling, mill 128, 146
Balls, Farling, mill & store 128
Barker, Nathan 154
Barton, Benjn. 118
Battersons, Henry, plantation 194
Battson, James 53
Baxter, William 61
Baxter, Wm. 61
Bayley, Joseph 176
Bayley, Pearce 176
Bayly, Joseph 176
Bayly, Peirce 176
Beaty, Andrew 95
Beaty, Jeames 95
Beaty, Robert 97
Beaver Dam 176, 190
Beaver Dam Branch of Goose Creek 118
Beaver Dam, old ford 190
Beavers, Thomas 166
Beavers, William 95, 97
Beavers, Wm. 144
Belhaven 114
Bennet, Jeames 95, 97
Berkley, William 85
Berkley, Wm. 136
Berkleys, Wm., spring branch 85
Best, James 148, 172, 210
Best, John 71
Betwixt the Hills 103
Bewley, Anthony 118
Binns 182
Binns, Charles, Clerk of the Court 1, 3, 13, 23, 31, 43, 47, 61, 65, 76, 78, 91, 99, 101, 112, 114, 140, 142, 148, 158, 162, 164, 172, 174, 176, 186, 192, 196, 200, 208
Binns, John 210
Bishop, John 122, 210
Bishop's, land 122
blacksmith's shop 194
Blue Ridge 11, 101, 109, 111, 124
Bodines, Isaac 190
Bohen, Joseph 128
Boiles, John 144
Bollin, George, drain of 178
Bonds, John, lot 73
Boorom, William 118
Booth, John 45
Bordine, Cornels. 107
Bowlings, George 174
Braddock Road 111
Braddock, Ralf 9
Bradleys spring-house 184
Bradleys, Jonas, field 184
Broad Run 17, 57, 144, 188
Broad Run, other 41
Broad Run Bridge 19, 25, 89
Broad Run Church 126, 140, 150
Broadwater, J. 196
Bronaugh, Capt. William 176
Bronaugh, William 158
Bronaugh, Wm. 156
Brookes, William 164, 166
Brown, H. 132
Brown, Henry 132
Brown, J. 93

Brown, John 73, 105
Brown, John, and others, mill of 91
Brown, Mercer 132, 138
Brown, Merser 91
Brown, William 76, 91, 138, 148
Brown, Willm. 76
Brown, Wm. 87, 91
Brown's, Dawson, plantation 176
Brown's, Dawson, wheat field 176
Brown's, Henry, plantation 132
Brown's, Mercer, dwelling-home 132
Brown's, Mercer, land 122
Buchannan, William 43
Buchener, William 51
Bull Run 63
Bull Run Mountains 85
Burck, John 53
Burson, Benja. 73
John Burk 53

C
Caldwell, John 210
Caldwell, Joseph 210
Caldwell, Moses 210
Caldwell's, Joseph, land 164
Calwell, Joseph 166
Cameron Parish 150
Cameron Parish, Vestry 150
Canarys, R. 5
Canbeys road 200
Canby, Samuel 118
Canby's, Saml., mill 118
Canbys mill 118
Carnahan, Adam 166
Carolina Road 182, 186
Carr, Peter 206, 208, 210
Carr's, Peter, house 206
Carrs dwelling-house 210
Carter & Ellzey, line of 204
Carter & Flood, line of 204
Carter, James 124
Carter, Peter 43, 61
Carters corner 204
Carters line 204
Catoctan, mouth of 80
Cavens, John 71, 87 109

Cavin, Mr. 170
Cavin's, William, plantation 164
Cavin's, Wm., Land 164
Cavins 164
Cavins, John 71, 172
Cavins, William 166, 170
Cavins, Wm. 166
Cellum, Emanewel 118
Champ, John 23
Chandler, Benjamin 136
Chandler's, Benjamin, plantation 136
Chandlers, Benja. 136
Chandlers, Benja., plantation 85
Chinn, Elijah 69
Chinn, Thomas 156, 158
Chinn, Thos. 53
Chinn's, Elijah, old field 39
Chinns, Christr., plantation 53
Chinns, Elijah, line 53
Chinns, Thomas, plantation 53
Church Road 126
Church, near Mountain Road 156, 158
Church, new 150
Cime, Henry 178
Clapham, J. 101
Clapham, Josias 9, 27, 134
Clapham's, Josias, plantation 134
Clapham's, Josias, orchard 134
Claypole, James 208, 210
Claypoole, James 208
Clearys, Ben., land 200
Clews, Thomas 3
Clice, John 109
Cockerile, Benjamin 192
Cockerile, Sandford 192
Cockerill, Benja. 37, 192
Cockerill, Sandford 192
Cockerill, Sanford 37, 192
Cockrell, Thomas 142
Cogill, Isaac 124
Colchester 57
Coleman, James, Gent. 196
Coleman, Jas., Gent. 196
Coleman, Jno. 140
Coleman, John 118

Coleman, Joseph 166
Colwell, John 166
Colwell, Joseph 170
Colwell, Mr. 170
Colwells, Mr., land 170
Combses, Widow, field 190
Comings, Malakiah 124
Compton, Saml. 73
Compton, Samuel 73, 76
Connell, Thomas 13
Conrad, John 184
Conrad, Jonathan 184
Cooks, James, house 198
Cookses, James 198
Coombs, Andrew 118
Cooper, Spencer 118
Cotton, John 180, 182
Cotton, William 29
Cotton, Wm., Senr. 152
County Line 39
County Line 39, 168
County Road 190
County Road to Vestals Gap 130
Courthouse 61
Cox, Majr. Saml. 204
Coxes Land 204
Coxes Mill 204
Coxs, Harmon, land 105
Craig, James 210
Craven 61
Craven, (?) 144
Creek, above mill dam 184
Crupper, Richard 190, 194
Cumins, Joseph 124
Curtis, John 192
St. Clair, John 134

D
dam 178
Daniel, Joshua, Gent. 198
Danils, Sons, field 168
Davis, Abraham 210
Davis, Jas. 204
Davis, John 63
Davis, John, land of 122
Dawdle, George 95, 97

Dawson's 160
Dawson's Ford 1, 160
Dawson's Jno., plantation 1
Dehaven, Abrm. 33
Dehaven, William 45
Deurin, George 97
Difficult Bridge 196
Difficult Hill 188
Dodd, John 87, 206, 208
Donaldson, Stephen 160
Donaldson, Stephen, Gent. 61
Dorsitt, John 146
Douglass, William 148, 174, 198, 202
Douglass, William, Gent. 146
Douglass, Wm. 89, 146, 198
Douglass, Wm., Gent. 89
Doutys 210
Dowdalls, John, mill road 188
Dowdles, John, mill 188
Downs, John 95, 97
Drake, Thomas 124
Drakes, Thomas, meadow 176
Drakes, Thos., meadow 124
Dugliss, Wm. 160
Duncan, Joshua 200
Dunkin, Joshua 200
Dunlap, John 124
Durin, George 95
Dwelling house 204

E
Edwards, B., road 202
Edwards, Benjn. 202
Edwards, Philip 210
Elgin, Francis 47, 152, 160
Elgin, Frans. 47, 55
Ellzey & Carter, line 204
Ellzeys land 204
Elzey's, Mr., plantation 1
Emery, Geo. 210
Eskridge, Chas. 13
Evans, Joshua 140
Evans's, Joshua, shop 140
Evens, Even, land 103
Evens's shop 126

Everharts, Jacob, mill 41
Everheart's mill 41
Evins, Joshua 126

F
Fairey, John 109
Fairfax County 196
Fairfax County, Commissioners 196
Fairfax Esq., Honorable George Wm., land 109
Fairfax's, Hon'ble George William, land 101
Fairfax's, Honorable George Wm., land 103
Fairhurst, Jeremiah 3
Farrows, Joseph, old place 194
Farrows, Joseph, mouth of lane 194
Fauntleroy, Bushrod 13
Fauq. County Line 85
Fauquier, Court of 85
Feagan, Dan 204
Ferguson, Francis 59
Ferguson, Henry 73
Fergusons 59
ferry 80
ferry road 27, 164, 202
ferry road, gate 202
Fiedler, William 23
Field, Wm. 186
Fields, William 186
Fitzsimmons plantation 156
Flood & Carter, line of 204
Floods, Thomas, land 204
Forkeson, James 41
Fouch, Isaac 47, 55, 160
Fox, Amos 37
Fred, Joseph 124
Freizell, Jacob 124
French, James 146
Frier, Robert, Gent. 196

G
Gallahans road 184
Gap Road 59
Gardner, Sylvester 78
Garner, (?) 85

Garrett 156
Garrett, Thomas 200
George Town 1
George, Thos. 33
George's, Thos., land 134
Georges, John, mill 174
Gest, Thomas 210
Gibson, Issac 114, 116
Gibson, John 124
Gibson, Joseph 114, 116
Gibson, Moses 124
Gibson, Mr. 162
Gibson, Thomas 124
Gibson's, John, road 168
Gibsons, John, mill 162
Gipsons field 168
Gipsons Land 168
Gipsons, John, mill 168
Going, George 33
Goodwin, Amos 122
Goose Creek 118, 124, 156, 160, 176, 194
Goose Creek Meetinghouse 87
Goose Creek, Dawson's ford 160
Goose Creek, ford of 176, 194, 204
Goose Creek, Morris's ford 160
Goose Creek, Southwest Fork 156
Gore 59, 65
Gore, Jos. 103
Gore, Josa. 73
Gore, Josha. 122
Gore, Joshua 59, 65, 67, 76, 99, 101, 105, 122
Gore, Thomas 65
Gore, Thos. 67
Gore's, Joshua, lane 73
Gragg, John, land of 105
Grahams field 184
Grahams, Peter 184
Grant, John, land 105
Grayson, Benjamin, Gent. 1
Great Mountain Road 78
Great Road 5, 45, 114, 118
Great Road, main 170
Great Spring 198
Greenup, Ch. 204

Greenup, Christe. 178
Greenup, Christo. 178, 180, 182
Gregg, Richard 146
Gregg, Robert 146
Gregg, Saml. 120
Gregg, Samuel 49, 120, 146
Gregg, Thos. 190, 200
Gregg, Thos., potter 118
Gregg, William 166
Greggs, Thos. 190
Grens, John 188
Griggs, Thomas, potter 118
Griggs, Thos., meadow 200
Gurly, Zacariah 45
Guy, Hezekiah 124
Guy, Samuel 124
Guys, Hezekiah, grist-mill 124

H
Haddocks, John 95
Hadocks, John 97
Hagerman, Abram. 194
Hague, Francis 170
Hague, Thomas 210
Hague's, Francis, land 170
Hail, James 124
Hails road 194
Hall, John 63, 85, 204
Hamilton 164
Hamilton, Col. James, field 172
Hamilton, James 87, 109, 112, 128
Hamilton, James, Gent. 71
Hamilton, Jas. 76, 91, 138, 172
Hamilton, Majr. James 19, 25
Hampton, Jeremiah 39
Hancks, Simon 176
Hancock, Simon 150
Hanks, William 49
Hanks, Wm. 49
Harbart, Peter 210
Harbour 182
Harbour, P. 182
Harper's Ferry 103
Harpers, Robt., ferry 103
Hart's, Joseph, house 122
Hatcher, William 91

Heales, George, quarter 39
Heaton, Moses 128
Heatton, John 128
Heatton, Moses 128
Henry, David 210
Henry, John, Jun. 210
Hibbs, Jacob, field 120
Hibs, Joseph 146
Hiegley, Jobe 188
Hieugley, Jacob 188
Hill, Saml. 109
Hill, William 146
Hils, Joseph 45
Hixson, Timothy 73, 210
Hoff, Benjamin 103
Hoff, John 144
Hoff, Philip 73
Hoge, Joseph 124
Hoker, Jeames 97
Holand, Jerrol 146
Hole, Charles 109
Hollingsworth's, Rachel, plantation 21
Horseman, Wm. 140
Horsman, William 126, 140
Horsman's fence 126
Hough, Benjn. 101
Hough, John 19, 89
Hough's mill 17, 89
Hough's, Saml., mill 180
Houghs mill 180, 182
Houghs, Wm., mill 182
Houghton, Elijah 146
house, miller's dam 168
house, new 168
Howel, Timothy 105
Hubbell, Thomas 144
Huff, Benjamin 101
Huff, John 95, 97
Huguly, Abraham 180
Hugulys fence 180
Hugulys, Abraham 180
Humphrey, Thomas 73
Humphreys, John 166
Humphreys, Thomas 59, 210
Hunsman, Peter 210

Hutchison, Jeremiah 93, 150
Hutchison, Joseph 95, 97
Hutton, Joseph 146
Hyinman, Mathew 166

I
Iden's, Samuel, land 122
Ireland, Andw. 210
Irwin, Samuel 134
Isemans mill 184
Isemans mill road 184
Isermans road 184

J
Jackson, Alexis 45
James, John 210
Jamieson, Robert 97, 101
Jamieson, Robt. 122
Jamison, Robert 101, 122
Jamison, Robt. 97, 103, 105, 109
Janney, Abel 21, 146
Janney, William 3, 76
Janney, Wm. 76
Janney's, Jacob, mill 5
Janney's, Joseph, mill 200
Janney's, Mahlon, mill 21, 45, 148, 164, 166
Janneys mill 200
Janneys, Jacob, mill 76
Jannys, Malon, mill 170
Jeney's, Abel, road 49
Jennings, James 43
Jenny's, Abel, road 146
John, Thomas 33, 35
Johns, Thomas 33
Johnson, Tunes 95, 97
Jones Road 182
Jones, Jacob 45
Jones, Jas. 166
Jones, John 31, 180, 182, 204
Jones, Thos. 109
Jones, William 27

K
Kirk, William 7

Kirk's, Wm., mill 80
Kirk's Wm. Grist-mill 9
Kirkbride, Mahlon, land 122
Kirks mill 83
Kirks, William, mill 83
Kitockton Meetinghouse 87
Kittockton Mountain 164
Kittocton Creek, old ford 122
Knowland, Mr., ferry 170

L
Lacey & Moore, line 204
Lacey, J. 204
Lacey, Joseph 204
Lacey's, Joseph, plantation 204
Laceys land 204
Lacock, Nathan 210
Lafevers 182
Lake, Thom. 95, 97, 144
Lampkin, James 136
Lampkins, James, plantation 85
Lane, Capt. James 13
Lane, Har. 192
Lane, Jas. 93
Lane, Jas., Gent. 17
Lane, William Carr, Gent. 37
Lane's mill 37
Lane's store 37
Lane's, Capt. James, mill 13
Lasswell's ford 15, 23, 29
Laycocks, Willm., field 41
Lechus, Pal 168
Lee 182
Lee's burg 15, 55
Leesburg 5, 29, 63, 73, 76, 99, 112, 160, 164, 188, 202, 206, 208
Leesburg and Winchester Road 63
Leesburg Road 190
Leesburgh 3, 5, 9, 27, 35, 45, 89, 105, 122, 134
Leesburgh to Snicker's Road 122
Leith, James 69, 124
Leith's, Jas., road 69
Lemons, John 124
Lewelion, Thomas 103
Lewis, Abram 168

Lewis, George 73
Lewis, James 162, 168
Lewis, Jno. 57
Lewis, John 57, 61, 89, 164, 202
Lewis, Stephen 73
Lewis, Thomas, Gent. 47, 176
Lewis, Thos. 29, 47, 55, 114, 150, 162, 176
Lewis, Vincent 1, 37, 144
Lewis's, John, lane 61
Lister, John 27
Little River 85, 95, 107
Little River, ford of 107
Loudoun County, Commissioners 196
Loudoun Road 78
Lous, J. 168
Lovatt, Daniel 120
Love, Saml. 93
Love, Samuel 93
Lovet's, Danil, plantation 49

M
Ma____, Thomson, Esq. 164
MacCartys, Thaddeus, house 194
Maffitt, Josiah 154
Mahonah 190
Mahonahs fence 190
Mahonnahs, James, fence 190
Main Road, bridge on 9
Mann, George 132
Manning, Edmund 45
Marbury, Thomas 156, 158
March, John 210
Marks, Elisha 122, 210
Marks, John 73
Marks, Thos. 210
Martins, James 118
Maryland, road in 80
Mason, Benj. 142
Mason, Benjamin 1 42
Mason, Thompson, Esq. 198
Mason, Thompson, Esq., land 61
Mason, Thompson, Esq., plantation 61
Mason, Thompson, Esq., quarter of 198
Mason's, Mr., land 164
Masons, Thompson, mill 71
Massey, Mr. 27
Massey's, Lee, fence 27
Matheny, Daniel 146
Matheny, Wm. 146
Mathew, Simon 109
Mathews, Simon 103
Mathews, Thomas 118
Mays, Lanord, fence 128
McChristey, Artha 109
McClain, John 186
McClan, William 186
McClellan, William 186
McClellans, Mr., road 186
McCullys, Robert, tan-house 190
McGeach 156
McGeach, John 210
McGeeith, James 200
McIlhaney, John 120
McIlhanney, Jno. 120
Mcilheney, John 49
McIlheney, Squire 21
McNabb's, William, house 156
McNabb's, William, plantation 156
Mead 182
Mead, William 31, 47
Mead, Wm. 31, 55, 89, 160
Meads, Wm. 180
Meads, Wm., meadow 55
Meetinghouse 71
Megeach, James 118
Megeach, Joseph 166
Megeath, James 200
Mercer, James 107
Mercer's, James, plantation 107
MiCarty, Thaddeus 194
Michael, Henry 130
Michaels, Daniel 174
Michel, Henry, land 103
Mikel, Dan 178
Mikil, Henory 130
mill 111
mill branch, mouth of 194
mill dam 184

mill path 188
mill race 184
mill road 51
Millers, Peter 174, 178
Millers, Peter, field 178
Millers, Valentine 103
Millstone Road 184
Milner, Joseph 118
Mine Branch 188
Minor, Colo. 31
Minor, Nich. 1, 3, 25, 31
Minor, Nich., Gent. 51
Minor, Nicholas, Gent. 31, 43, 51
Minor, Nichs. 160
Minor's, Nicholas, plantation 43
Misal, J___ief 109
Molton, Wm. 166
Monkhouse, Jonathan 55
Monkhouse, Jonathan, corner-tree 55
Monkhouses fence 55
Moore 204
Moore, John 204
Moores land 204
Morin's, Widow, field 85
Morlans, Steven, field 182
Morris's ford 160
Morris's, Jno., plantation 37
Morrison, James 118
Morrison, William 170
Morrison, Wm. 164
Moss, John 1, 31
Moss, John 150
Mount, Tho. 190
Mountain Road 144, 156, 158, 200
Mountain Road 9, 13, 37, 93
Mountain Road, leading to Colchester 57
Mounts, Thos. 190
Mourhead, William 210
Mucelhaney, Jno., Gent. 49
Muls, David 49
Murry, Archibald 146
Myers, Jonathan 112, 122

N

Neafus, George 210
Neal, William 124
Neals Heirs 93
Neilson, John 210
Newhouse, David 109
Nichols 200
Nichols, Isaac 65, 67, 210
Nichols, Isaac, Jr. 65
Nichols, Isaac, Junior 122
Nichols, James 73
Nichols's, Isaac, mill 87
Nichols's, William, land 122
Nickol's, Isaac, mill 76
Niles, Samuel 124
Nixon, George 210
Nixon's mill 180
Nixon's, George, lane 49
Nixons line 182
Nixons mill 182
Nixons wheat field 120
Nixons, Geo. 120
Nixons, Mr. George, mill 180, 182
Noland, Phil 25, 27, 33
Noland, Phil., Gent. 146
Noland's ferry 134
Noland's ferry road 134
Nolands ferry 27, 35, 164
Norman, George 21
Northwest Fork 118

O
Olakers, John 124
Olakers, William 124
Old Abbet, plantation of 61
Old Ox Road 51
Oldacris mill 124
Oldakers, William 124
Orason, Andrew 112
Orison, Andrew 122
Orisson, John 206
Orr, John 142
Osbirn, Nicolus 73
Osborn lane 103
Osborn, John 103
Osborn, John, Senior, fence 103
Osborn, John, Sr. 101

Osborn, Nicholas 11, 99
Osburn, John, Junior 109
Osburn, John, Senior 109
Osburn, John, Senior, road 111
Osburn, Richard 109, 210
Owsley, Mr. 176
Owsley, T. 168
Owsley, Thomas 176
Owsley, Thos. 162, 168
Owsley's, Mr., still-house 176
Owsleys Branch 204
Ox Road 37, 51, 192
Oxley, Henry, Junior 41
Oxley, Henry, Junr. 166
Ozbourns house 59
Ozbourns, John 59
Ozbourns, Richard 59

P
Page's, Mr., land 164
Pains ferry 49
Pains, Frail, ferry 45
Pancoast, Israel 210
Parker, Joseph 118
Patterson, Flemg. 89
Patterson, Fleming 89
Patterson, Fleming, Gent. 160
Patterson, Flemming 99
Pearce, Lewis 107
Perce, Griffy 210
Perces, John, land 103
Petters, Junis 146
Peyton, Craven 15, 61, 154, 164
Peyton, Craven, Gent. 29
Peyton, Francis 23, 134, 156
Peyton, Frans. 150
Peyton, Fras., Gent. 59, 107
Peyton's, Craven, lot 122
Peyton's, Craven, meadow 122
Phillips, John 146
Phillips, Nicklis, field 41
Pickett's, John, land 122
Pierce, John 73, 76
Piet, John, Sen. 210
Piles, John 124, 140
Piles's, Richard, plantation 51

Piney Branch 95, 144
Po____, Benjamin, meadow 122
Pole bridge 202
Pool, Benjamin 65, 67
Pools, Benjamin, plantation 112
Popkins, plant(ation) 9
Popkins, Robt., fence 9
Potomack River 11
Pott's mill 101
Potts mill 103, 109
Potts, David 109
Potts, Ezeikle, land 103
Potts, Ezekiel 109
Potts, Nathan 109
Potts, Nathan, land 103
Potts, saml. 122
Potts, Samuel 101, 109, 122
Powell, Leven 69, 105
Powell, Leven, Gent. 85
Powell's, Leven, mill 176
Powells mill 107, 124
Powells mill road 85
Powells, Leven, mill 124, 136
Powells, Leven, mill road 136
Powells, Leven, plantation 53
Powells, Levin, mill 176
Prince William line 204
Prince William, road to 13
Pursell, Thomas 120
Pursell, Thos. 120
Pursley, Thomas 99, 122, 130
Pursley, Thos. 73, 105, 122
Pursleys, Thomas, land 103

Q
Quaker Meetinghouse 124, 146, 164
Quakers 148
Quarter Branch 178
Quik, Casper 109

R
Race ground 144
Ramey, Jacob 13, 93
Rameys, Abslom 176
Rasberry Plane 61
Ratekin, James 71

Read's, Jacob, fence 156
Read's, Jacob, plantation 156
Reads, Jacob 156
Reed, Jacob 23, 78, 85
Reeder, Daniel 144
Reeder, David 95, 144
Reeder, Joseph 95, 144
Reeder's, Joseph and Daniel, lines 144
Reedor, Daniel 97
Reedor, David 97
Reedor, Joseph 97
Rees, David, blacksmith shop of 194
Reid, Jacob 107, 158
Remey, Jacob 13
Respas, Thomas 198
Respess, Thomas 198, 202
Reynolds, Richard 45
Rhodes's, Moses, path 55
Rice, William 118
Richardson, Jonathan 21
Richardson, Joseph 67
Ringo, Henry 63, 95, 97
Roach, Richard 7
Roach's mill 41
Roach's, Richard, mill 7
Road, new 111, 130
Roberson, Robert 45
Roberts, Owen 87
Roberts, Richd. 7, 9
Roberts, William 208
Roberts, Wm. 208
Robinson, W. 176
Robinson, William 162, 168, 176
Robnson, Wm. 168
Roch, James 166
Roch, Richd., mill of 132
Rocheas, Richard, mill 41
Rodgers, Thomas 210
Rogers, Hamilton 208
Ross, Alexander 146
Ross, William 1
Roszel, Stephen 200
Roszell, Stephen 200
Round Hill 5

Rusel, John, land 103
Russel, Capt. Anthony 144
Russel's, Capt., line 144
Russell, A. 144
Russell, Anthony 142
Russell, Anthy. 144
Russell, Tho. 124
Russell, Thomas 124
Rust, Benj. 136
Rust, W. 176
Rust, William 114, 124, 176

S
Sanders path 194
Sanders, Isaac 118, 156
Sanders, James 194
Sanders, Jas. 134
Sands, Isaac 132
Saunders's, Philip, plantation 61
saw mill 182
Schawen, Isaac 166
Schooley, John 112
Schooley, Saml. 128
Schooley, William 170
Schooley, Wm. 170
Schooley's, F., land 164
Schooley's, Wm., land 164
Scooleys spring drain 41
Scooleys, Samuel 41
Scooling, Francis 109
Selfs, Charnick 188
Settlement 166
Shaffers, Geo., lot 120
Shanks, Conard 109
Shaver 49
Sheepards, Thomas, mill 105
Shepard land 105
Shepard mill 99
Shepard, Thos. 105
Shoemaker, Jacob 120
Shoemakers, Jacob, barn 120
Shoemakers, Jacob, field of barley 120
Shoemakers, Jacob, lane 120
Shores, Thomas 186

Short Hill 11
Shover, Adam 174, 178
Shover, William 174
Shreave, Benjn. 55
Shreeve, Benja. 47
Shreeve's, Benjn., plantation 1
Shreeve's, Wm., plantation 1
Shreeves, Ben. 210
Shreive, Benjamin 47
Shreve, William 210
Shugarland Meetinghouse 188
Shugerland Run 124
Simons, Luwis 168
Sinkler, John 146
Skooley, John 122
Slaughs, Phillip 59
Slaught, Phillip 73
Smarr, John 63, 78, 204
Smith, Andrew 210
Smith, David 27
Smith, John 210
Smith, Nathanial 186
Smith, Samuel 65, 67
Smith, Thomas 124
Smith, Weathers 192
Smith, William 45
Smith, William, Gent. 176
Smith, Wm. 114, 150
Smith's road 192
Smith's shop 144
Smith's, Samuel, plantation 41
Smiths, James 124
Snedcker, Garrat 95
Snedcker, Garret 97
Snicker's 78, 122
Snicker's Gap 85
Snickers Gap 122
Snickers Gap Road 85
Snickers's Gap 107
Sniggars Gap 118
Snigger's Gap 76
Sorrell, Thomas 1
Spencer, Nathan 5, 122, 148
Spencer's, Nathan, goose pond 122
spring-head 122

Spurr, Richard 124
Spurr, Richd. 140
Squires, George 210
Stadlers house 204
Stall, John 78
Stanhope, William, Gent. 196
Stanhope, Wm. 196
Starks, Thomas 31
Steer, James 83
Steer, John 83
Steer, John & James 83
Steere, Jno. 166
Steere, John 33
Stephens, James 61
Stephens, James, plantation 61
Stephens, Richard 17
Stephens, William 114
Stephens, Wm. 114, 116
Stephens, Wm. 39
Stevens, James 166
Stevens, Thomas 166
Stone, Henry 146
Stump, John 45
Stump, Thomas 45
Sugarland Run 150
Summers, G. 93
Summers, George, Gent. 93
Swanck, Larrance 109

T
Taler, George 152
Tates, Wm., land 105
Tavener, George 138
Tavener, George 148
Tavenner, Geo. 148
Taverner, George 91
Taylor, Geo. 29
Taylor, George 152
Taylor, John 190
Taylors, Henry, field 69
Taylors, Henry, house 69
Taylors, Henry, large gate 69
Taylors, Henry, little gate 69
Taylors, Henry, pasture 69
Taylors, Henry, plantation 69
Taylors, Henry, road to mill 69

Taylors, Henry, still-house 69
Thacher, Richard 73
Thachers lane 105
Thachers, Richard 105
Thatchers, Richard 99
Thomas, Jason 134
Thomas, Jos. 33, 35
Thomas, Joseph 33, 41
Thomas, Moses 210
Thompson, Andrew 146, 166
Thompson, Isaac 122
Thompson, Israel 109
Thompson, Israel, his lane 122
Thompson's mill 122
Thompson's, Israel, mill 73
Thompsons mill 112
Thompsons, Israel, mill 112, 120, 122
Thomson, I. 109
Thomsons, Isral, mill 49
Thomspsons, Israel, mill 91
Tingle, George 122
Tobin, James 21, 146
Tobin, Thomas 146
Todds, Robert, lot 73
Todhunter Jno. 166
Todhunter, John 33, 35, 146
Tole, Jonathan 53
Tools, Jonathan, house 194
Topes, Henry 41
Town 61
Townsend's, Thomas, late lot 122
Townsends, Thomas, lot 73
Tramell, Samson 188
Tramels, John, tract of land 134
Trammell, John 9
Trammell's, John, fence 27
Trammell's, John, mill 27
Trammells rolling-road 188
Trenary's Run 47
Trenarys fence 55
Trenarys Run 55
Triplet, Col. 204
Triplet, Simon, Gent. 158
Triplets, Col., mill 190
Triplets, Francis 190
Triplett, Francis 156

Triplett, S. 190
Tripletts mill 56, 158
Tripletts mill road 190
Tripletts, Colonel Simon, mill 194
Tripletts, S., mill 194
Truax, John 210
Turley's, Sampson, plantation 144
Turner, Fielding 95, 142
Tuscarora 154
Tuskarora 154
Tyler, Jn. 204

U

V
Valandingham, Richr. 188
Valentine quarter 128
Valindine quarter 128
Van Horns, Bernard, field 194
Vanbuskirk, Isaac 174, 178
Vanbuskirk's, Isaac, field 41
Vansikkel, Gilbirt 118
Veale, William 43
Veale, Wm. 51
Vestal 109
Vestal Gap 109
Vestal, John 109
Vestals Gap 101, 103, 130, 180
Vestals Gap Road 180
Vincels, Adam 41

W
Waldin, John 97
Waldin, Willm. 97
Walker, Isaac 118
Walker, John 194
Warford, Abram 144
Warfords, Abraham, Line 144
Warfurd, Abra. 144
Warfurd, John 76
Wattson, Richard 206
Wells, Jacob 166
West, Capt. Thomas 204
West, Charles 63, 124
West, Geo., Gent. 51
West, Majr. Charles 204

West, Majr. Charles, line of 204
West, Thomas 97, 114, 162
West, Ths. 168
West's ordinary 78, 85
Wests, Capt. Thomas 204
Wests, Geo., lane 152
Wests, Majr. Charles, land 204
Wests, T. 168
Wests, Thos. 116
Whaley, James 124, 140
Whaley, John 192
Whealey, James 17
White Ridge 51
White, Josiah, Jun. 210
White, Mathew 188
Whitely, William 29
Whitely, Wm. 152
Wiet's, Edwart, house 49
Wiet's, Edwart, plantation 49
Wigington, Spensor 188
Wikeoffs, Saml., spring 95
Wildman, Jacob 210
Wildman, William 112
Wildman, Wm. 122, 210
Wilks, Francis 3, 31
Willets 190
William's Gap 5
William's Gap Road 59
Williams Gap 99
Williams, David, land 103
Williams, Jinkin 132
Williams, John 206
Williams, R. 132
Williams, Widow 156
Williams's Gap 3, 112
Wilson, John 73
Wilson, Joseph 210
Winchester 63, 206, 208
Wittcre, John 73
Wolard, William 41
Wolf, John 184
Wollards, Wm., fence 27
Woodley, Benjamin 210
Woolard, William 41, 134, 166
Wren 182
Wren, Jno. 196

Wyatt, Edward 45
Wyckoff, Saml. 95, 97
Wyckoff, Samuel 63, 95
Wycoff, Saml. 95, 97

X-Y-Z
Yeldell, Robert 11

Roberto Costantino

Life is, in looking back, very much in the tradition of a Henry James novel. He was born in Bangkok, Thailand, the scion of an American Foreign Service Officer and Wife. In his formative years he lived in, also, Washington, D.C., Guatemala City, Guatemala, Buenos Aires, Argentina, Washington, D.C., again, before his family settled in Fairfax County, Virginia. He earned his High School Diploma from Langley High School, McLean. He went to college at Indiana University, Bloomington, and graduated from Loyola University, New Orleans, Bachelor of Arts, 1980. Afterwards, Roberto was awarded a Certificate of Accounting from the School of Continuing Education, The American University, Washington, D.C. Roberto worked for thirteen years in the financial services industry as an insurance agent and broker, registered representative, before the economy drove him out of business. Then he went to graduate school at the University of Virginia, Charlottesville, in the School of Architecture, Department of Urban and Environmental Planning, whereat he earned a Master of Planning with a Concentration in Preservation Planning, 1996. Roberto authored a reference book recording a historical landscape site entitled Israel Thompson's Plantation, Loudoun County, Virginia, under the direction of Professor K. Edward Lay, and published by the University of Virginia, School of Architecture, 1994. Roberto is a retail merchant who specializes in Virginia art and antique objects and a Loudoun County School System Department of Transportation employee. Roberto and his Wife and children live in "Hutton's Messuage", Loudoun County, since 1987.

www.ingramcontent.com/pod-product-compliance
Lightning Source LLC
Chambersburg PA
CBHW081146230426
43664CB00018B/2819